A SHORT GUIDE TO PROCUREMENT RISK

SHORT GUIDES TO BUSINESS RISK, THE SERIES

Risk is a far more complex and demanding issue than it was ten years ago. Risk managers may have expertise in the general aspects of risk management and in the specifics that relate directly to their business, but they are much less likely to understand other more specialist risks. Equally, Company Directors may find themselves falling down in their duty to manage risk because they don't have enough knowledge to be able to talk to their risk team, in a sensible way.

The short guides to risk are not going to make either of these groups experts in the subject but will give them plenty to get started and in a format and an extent (circa 100 pages) that is readily digested.

Titles in the series will include:

- *A Short Guide to Reputation Risk* (published)
- *A Short Guide to Fraud Risk* (published)
- *A Short Guide to Ethical Risk*
- *A Short Guide to Customs Risk*
- *A Short Guide to Kidnap and Ransom Risk*
- *A Short Guide to Political Risk*
- *A Short Guide to Operational Risk*
- *A Short Guide to Equality Risk*
- *A Short Guide to Facilitating Risk Management*

Visit www.gowerpublishing.com/shortguidestorisk for details of the latest titles, sample chapters and help on requesting a standing order.

A Short Guide to Procurement Risk

Richard Russill

GOWER

Published by
Gower Publishing Limited
Wey Court East
Union Road
Farnham
Surrey GU9 7PT
England

Gower Publishing Company
Suite 420
101 Cherry Street
Burlington, VT 05401-4405
USA

www.gowerpublishing.com

British Library Cataloguing in Publication Data
Russill, Richard, 1943-
  A short guide to procurement risk. -- (Short guides to
  business risk)
  1. Industrial procurement. 2. Risk management.
  I. Title II. Series
  658.7'2-dc22

  ISBN: 978-0-566-09218-3 (pbk)
  ISBN: 978-0-566-09219-0 (ebk)

Library of Congress Cataloging-in-Publication Data
Russill, Richard, 1943-
  A short guide to procurement risk / by Richard Russill.
    p. cm.
  Includes bibliographical references and index.
  ISBN 978-0-566-09218-3 (pbk.) -- ISBN 978-0-566-09219-0 (ebook)   1.
  Industrial procurement. 2. Risk management. I. Title.
  HD39.5.R873 2010
  658.7'2--dc22

                                                        2010000627

Mixed Sources
Product group from well-managed
forests and other controlled sources
www.fsc.org Cert no. SA-COC-1565
© 1996 Forest Stewardship Council
FSC

Printed and bound in Great Britain by
MPG Books Group, UK

Contents

List of Figures

Introduction

Do you like living dangerously? Then read this book: it exposes you to over seventy types of risk you can take in your business life. Want to live successfully? Then also read about the practical ways of mitigating them.

This book is for all business people, not just buyers and procurement specialists. As one CEO put it 'we buy things, we transform them and we sell, and we have to excel at all of that to be best.' So, if you're in business, you're in procurement. And if *that* is not widely known in your company then it is exposed to serious risks over and above the ones that normally concern people at the input side of business, such as disrupted supply chains or supplier bankruptcy.

The solutions in this book come with a warning. It is dangerous simply to paste remedies over a risk problem if its underlying causes remain undisturbed. When this happens, risks that we thought we'd fixed come back and bite again. Therefore I want this book to help you see beneath the surface of commercial business life so that Procurement Risk Management is sustained and systemic, rather than superficial and temporary. The book also provides key questions for you to ask which will help to probe things more deeply.

As you read, I hope you will discover how the Procurement Risk Management approach described transcends contingency planning and becomes instead a stimulus for superior competitive advantage. This route to high performance is as relevant and necessary in the public sector as it is in corporate life. Ice-hockey star Wayne Gretsky said that 'a good hockey player plays where the puck is. A great hockey player plays where the puck is going to be.' This book helps us to see where procurement risks are going to be and, just in case we miss one, improves our ability to handle the unexpected when it happens. I hope you enjoy this book ... but don't run the risk of not buying it!

Dick Russill
Pembrokeshire
Wales UK
www.Russill.com

① Procurement and Risk – The Big Picture

PROCUREMENT'S PLACE IN THE BUSINESS ... AND THE NEED TO GET IT RIGHT

Every business enterprise uses suppliers in one form or another. It is inherent in the business model. One enlightened CEO described her company's business in this way: 'we buy, we transform and we sell.' She added: '... and we need to be equally good at all of that if our business is to be as successful as possible.' In other cases it might be more accurate to say 'this is what we do and what we sell to our customers, and we use external sources (of whatever) to make it possible to do that.' In the public sector, the equation could be expressed as 'we buy, we add value and we deliver.' The point is that no company or public sector organisation is an island. Resources are needed at one end of the business just as customers are required at the other.

Traditional procurement is no stranger to risk management, witness any good company's approach to contract terms and conditions and supply planning. But things move on. Public and private sector organisations have outsourced activities previously conducted in-house; what were domestic supply chains now span the globe in search of low cost sources; and communications technologies have dramatically increased the possibility and appetite for rapid, constant change ... whilst also rendering a company's activities more transparent and open to public scrutiny.

Despite this, most companies are so focused on managing the people and assets employed in the business and on satisfying their customers that they fail realise what is going on behind them in their supply markets. And it is not all good news:

- Vulnerabilities in physical supply chains are poorly understood and managed. This has been identified as one of four emerging risk issues likely to impact in the years to come.[1] The recent capture by Somali pirates of a cargo ship serves as a stark lesson that this is no theoretical forecast and that the 'unimaginable' does happen. Increasing supplier bankruptcies coming in the train of the economic crisis only add to supply chain woes.

- High growth in the Chinese economy in 2007–08 drove huge price increases in commodity raw materials along with additional concerns about shortages of supplies for Western economies. Freak weather conditions in Brazil and India caused wholesale prices of sugar to hit a near 28-year high, up 80 per cent in 2009 alone. An expected knock-on effect will be a global shortage of sweeteners as big importers of sugar switch into them as a substitute.

---

1 *World Economic Forum Report*, January 2008, 'Global risks 2008'.

- Although its supplier had breached a contract, a customer company had to accept a court ruling in favour of the supplier because the buyer had not exercised the contract's termination clause in a timely manner.[2]

- The value of procurement fraud in the UK increased by 347 per cent during 2008.[3]

- And truth continues to be stranger than fiction. Workers at a recently bankrupted French company supplying the car industry threatened to blow it up if their redundancy compensation claims were not satisfied. 'The gas bottles are in the factory. Everything is ready to blow it up,' said a union representative.[4]

Another company knew exactly what it was doing in its supply market but was caught for manipulating supplier behaviour.[5] The computer chip manufacturer was found guilty of engaging in illegal practices, one being to make payments to suppliers to halt or delay the launch of products containing competitors' components.

The view that supply chain vulnerability is an ongoing concern is confirmed by the fact that Aon's 2009 Global Risk Management Survey[6] includes supply chain failure in its Top Ten most pressing risks around the world. Interestingly at least half of the risks in the Top Ten can be directly related to procurement activity, and hence would fall within the remit of

---

2   *Supply Management*, 30 April 2009, 'Use it or lose it'.
3   *Supply Management*, 11 June 2009, 'The pressure is on'.
4   *The Daily Telegraph*, 14 July 2009. (The claim was settled without the need for detonation!).
5   *Supply Management*, 28 May 2009.
6   insight.aon.com *'The Definitive Report on Risk, 2009'*.

Procurement Risk Management (PRM).[7] One consequence of this is that procurement risk has emerged as a comprehensive topic in its own right rather than being a facet of specific but fragmented procurement tasks. The benefit of this 'promotion' up management's agenda is the requirement for more clarity about what is 'procurement risk' and greater awareness that risks can lurk in areas where traditionally they have not been sought.

However, a comprehensive commercially aware approach to procurement is not the norm. In its absence, organisations experience one or more of the harming events listed in Box 1 and will under-perform, maybe not survive, as a consequence. The impact of supply chain disruption on business performance has seldom been better described than in Hendricks and Singhal's comprehensive, and sobering, study of its effect on long-term shareholder value. To quote from their concluding summary:[8]

> *The evidence presented in this report makes a compelling case that ignoring the risk of supply chain disruptions can have serious negative economic consequences. Based on a sample of more than 800 supply chain disruption announcements, the evidence indicates that firms that suffer supply chain disruptions experience 33 to 40 per cent lower stock returns relative to their benchmarks, 13.5 per cent increase in share price volatility, 107 per cent drop in operating income, 7 per cent lower sales growth, and 11 per cent increase in costs. By any yardstick these are very significant*

---

7 In addition to supply chain failure the risks are: business interruption; commodity price risk; damage to reputation, and cash flow/liquidity risk.

8 Hendricks, K. and Singhal, V. 2005. *The Effect of Supply Chain Disruptions on Long-term Shareholder Value.*

economic losses. More importantly, firms do not quickly recover from these losses. The evidence indicates that firms continue to operate for at least two years at a lower performance level after experiencing disruptions. Given the significant economic losses, firms cannot afford such disruptions even if they occur infrequently.

BOX 1

WHAT ARE THE RISKS OF NO PROCUREMENT RISK MANAGEMENT?

- Profit, budgets, and cash flow are all hurt:
    - substantial reductions in shareholder value occur
    - need to maintain a far higher than necessary level of risk capital

- Customers kept waiting or turned down.

- Helplessness in dealing with supplier price increases.

- Output prices forced up with loss of competitiveness.

- Poor supplier performance or, worse, allocation or loss of supply.

- Fragmentation and loss of procurement negotiating leverage.

- Legally unsound contracts heavily biased in suppliers' favour.

- Unproductive use of human resources.

- Insufficient 'internal challenge' of specifications and decision-making.

- Decision-makers prey to the tactics of salespeople.

- Political embarrassment or damage to company image and reputation.

- Vulnerable to internal and external fraud.

- Exploited and manipulated by monopolies, cartels and hostile contractors.

- Supplier innovations passed to competitors.

- Beaten to the market by competitors with new products or services.

- Too quick or too late to market with own new offerings.

- Damage to brand and company reputation by unethical behaviour or incompetence.

- Organisation is penalised for non-compliance with regulatory requirements.

- Organisation's activities become subject of public scrutiny and investigation.

The ultimate goal of risk management is to protect and enhance what the enterprise is primarily there to do. In the private sector the aim is profitable survival. The public sector equivalent is to deliver maximum service and organisational effectiveness within the constraints of the resources provided to do it. This includes money. But is the risk-catching net being cast wide enough? Focusing on risks external to the company tells only half the story. What is less well known is that risk exposures also exist inside the company and can be just as damaging.

Whilst excellent articles are written about PRM, the balance of content trends in the direction of risk evaluation and mitigation rather than something which is arguably even more important, namely identifying risks at the outset. As one Chief Procurement Officer (CPO) observed: 'we are good at reacting to issues when they arise but not good at populating our risk register in the first place.'

'PLAYING WITH FIRE': THE ELEMENTS OF PROCUREMENT RISK MANAGEMENT

Procurement Risk exists for an organisation 'when supply market behaviour, and the organisation's dealings with suppliers, create outcomes which harm company reputation, capability, operational integrity and financial viability.'

The key word in this definition is 'harm'. This requires judgement, criteria, and maybe calculation, to decide if an event is potentially harmless or harmful. It is also necessary to distinguish between what is 'at risk' (that is, 'exposed') and the possible event that does the damage. For example, the company's ability to meet delivery commitments is exposed to the possibility of supply disruption or if a key supplier becomes bankrupt. Recessions mean that suppliers shut down production capacity to save overhead costs, which eventually lead to shortages when the upturn comes. Suppliers use price increases to ration supplies. Thus, financial performance and the ability to meet budgets is now exposed to the significant price increases that suppliers can impose when it is a seller's market.

In examining what was at risk, one public sector organisation addressed the question 'in what way could our work or existence be harmed if untamed risks escaped to do us damage?' Four main exposures were identified:

1. reputation;

2. operational continuity;

3. financial viability;

4. being a target for litigation.

The need to be clear about 'what is exposed' arises because, without it, it is difficult to work out what it is worth to reduce or prevent a risk from occurring. For example, the cost of a lost day of production is easily calculated. A possible disruptive event might be a strike at the haulage company that has the job of delivering production raw materials. The strike could feasibly last for five days. The contingency plan may be to hold a five-day stock of materials as insurance against the possibility of the strike. The cost of this plan can be compared with the cost of five days of lost production. If the contingency plan costs less than the impact of the strike then it makes sense to action the plan. An apparently cheaper option would be to hold the supplier responsible for the costs of non-delivery and seek to recover these afterwards. But this is reactive, will involve a lot of work to get the money back, and still leave a dissatisfied ultimate customer whose order has not been fulfilled. These indirect costs must be added into the total evaluation.

Another reason for taking pains to define exposures is that it helps to identify potential disruptive events. The usual approach is to say 'here is a supply chain ... what could go wrong with it, and what would be the cost of the harm done?' This convergent approach will identify possible events, but not as many as will be revealed by divergent thinking. The latter starts with an exposure ... e.g. reputation ... and then imagines all the supply-related things that could happen to tarnish it. 'Our reputation is exposed to the actions of others ... how many things can we think of that will damage our reputation if they happen?'

The combination of an exposure and an event is an 'impact'. If disruptive events happen and the company is exposed as previously mentioned, then the impacts are:

- tarnished reputation;

- interrupted day-to-day operations;

- spiralling costs;

- being sued.

Events actually have to happen to be harmful. But how likely are they to occur? Sophisticated mathematics can be used to estimate probability, but for most purposes 'high, medium or low' will often suffice, although the case for slightly more precision is made in Chapter 7. These terms can be quantified as follows:

- *high* means 'event will occur in most circumstances and one event can be expected each year.'

- *medium* means 'will probably occur at least once every five years.'

- *low* means 'not expected to occur in normal circumstances and less than once in every five years.'

Finally, what can be done to mitigate an undesirable impact caused by a high- or medium- probability event occurring? A mitigating action will reduce, eliminate, or compensate for the harm done and, in general, will involve either direct or indemnity actions. Direct action will reduce or eliminate the 'at risk' situation (e.g. by laying down some contingency stockholding), whereas indemnity actions are designed to 'let harm happen' but to provide compensation in the event (e.g. taking out insurance to cover business continuity).

The different elements of being 'At Risk' can be connected as follows:

$$\text{Being 'At Risk'} = \text{Impact} \times \text{Probability} \times \text{No Mitigation}$$

$$\text{where Impact} = \text{Exposure} \times \text{Event}$$

Just as fire is extinguished when either fuel, *or* oxygen, *or* temperature, is removed from a conflagration, so removing or reducing one or more elements in the above equation prevents being 'at risk'. However, effective PRM does include accepting some risks, with these situations being monitored to avoid being caught out if things change. Other situations can be left 'at risk' but contingency plans are ready should risks materialise. And where real trouble lurks, urgent action is required followed by regular audit.

TARGETING PRM IN THE RISK LANDSCAPE

Many definitions of risk management exist but are often too vague to be useful, such as 'risk is the probability of incurring loss or misfortune'. Most definitions focus only on the possibility of a disruptive event, such as a break in the supply chain, but what also matters is the failure to take advantage of an opportunity from which the organisation could benefit. This is recognised in the UK's Office of Government Commerce

(OGC) approach which defines risk as 'uncertainty of outcome, whether positive opportunity or negative impact.'[9]

As stated earlier in this chapter, procurement risk exists for an organisation 'when supply market behaviour, and the organisation's dealings with suppliers, create outcomes which harm company reputation, capability, operational integrity and financial viability.' This guide then defines Procurement Risk Management (PRM) as 'the name given to the measures taken ... including changes to behaviours, procedures and controls ... which remove procurement risks or reduce them to what is considered to be an acceptable level.'

There are a number of pre-requisites for risk identification to be effective. Two important ones are the already-discussed need to link an event to an exposure to quantify its impact, and the need for unbridled creativity in imagining potentially disruptive events in the first place. A comprehensive search for 'at risk' situations surveys five different landscapes where risks may lurk:

- external dependencies (e.g. supply chain robustness, supplier viability);

- market conditions and behaviours (e.g. competitive or not; supply availability);

- procurement process;

- management controls;

---

9   www.ogc.gov.uk *'Achieving Excellence, Guide 4: Risk and Value Management'*.

- ability and agility to handle unexpected events.

External Dependencies concerns the reliance on supply companies; their values and viability; performance, and the durability of supply chains. *Market Conditions and Behaviours* concerns the competitiveness or otherwise of supply markets; supply availability; price trends and the regulatory context. *Procurement Process* covers the way different people work together in all decision-making and behaviours which affect the customer's dealings with suppliers. *Management Controls* refers to the proper use of authority in the company; the framework whereby it is delegated and the principles expected to be employed. In effect this is the DNA of the procurement process. And the *Ability to Handle the Unexpected* means just what it says.

No one of the five risk landscapes is more important than the others. Figure 1.1 shows the 'Risk Catcher' which keeps the total risk management panorama in view, and the search process comprehensive. Importantly, this integrated approach encourages different risk specialists to come out of their silos of operation. For example, 'management controls' is usually the province of the company's Chief Internal Auditor; 'handling the unexpected' the concern of the Risk Director; and 'external dependencies' the focus of the CPO. These three do not often meet, but some joint risk catching gives them the reason to do so. The result of a shared risk analysis will be superior to the sum of its parts, with the bonus that non-procurement people have their eyes opened to the risks and opportunities presented by supply markets.

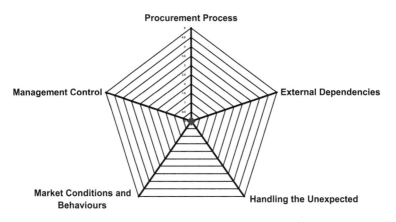

Figure 1.1   The 'Risk Catcher'

In the next five chapters, each of these risk landscapes is considered in more detail. We start with the subjects most often written about, namely, a company's dependence on external supply chains and its exposure to hostile market conditions. Then follow two less fashionable topics ... 'less fashionable' only because little is written about them. This may reflect the fact that they are not truly understood or that they are not held to be important. The opposite is true. Procurement Process and Management Controls are highly potent sources of risk, and all the more so if believed to be not relevant. The final topic deals with the occurrence of unexpected events and how some people and companies are better than others at handling them.

Each chapter provides examples of potential risks and what the remedies look like. Whilst this is useful, there is the danger that only the symptoms of problems will be fixed rather than their root causes. Hence, once the more concerning 'at risk' situations have been dealt with, it is important to make further changes which create a working climate and culture where PRM is a fact of day-to-day life rather than a specific task only revisited when the risk register needs updating. Thus the next five chapters also present the underlying principles of risk prevention appropriate to each risk landscape. These ensure a proactive approach to PRM where risks are less likely to materialise and do harm, as distinct from reactive PRM where disruptions are 'allowed' but where harm is prevented by the safety net of contingency plans or by being quick on one's feet.

When done well, a high-performance risk-aware procurement process provides the bonus of competitive advantage, with the ability to capitalise, rather than suffer, from the occurrence of unexpected events. This short guide explains how to do it. But before delving further, it is necessary to take stock of where an organisation currently stands vis-à-vis PRM best practice. Box 2 offers the means of a first self-assessment.

BOX 2

PROCUREMENT RISK MANAGEMENT: SELF-ASSESSMENT OF PRM PREPAREDNESS

Assess your company's PRM-preparedness by testing against the following criteria (1 = low, 5 = high)

Procurement Process

1. Procurement is non-existent as an identifiable defined process in the company.

2. Procurement behaviour is streetwise and deal-oriented but with little structure or functional influence.

Internal IT systems offer visibility of the supply chain.

3. Procurement activity is procedures-oriented and focused on internal customer service, albeit responsive to need.

Requisitions (timing and quantity) are driven by the company's daily operations' planning system.

IT systems have basic supplier information feeds and basic risk models are in place.

4. Procurement activity relies heavily on leverage and muscle-power.

Requirements are defined by the planning system and/or by commercially sensible considerations.

Decision-making is supported by analytical tools and an effective information system infrastructure.

IT systems provide real-time feeds on the status of goods within the supply chain.

5. Procurement is a core cross-company process integrated into the company strategy and designed to maximise sustained shareholder value. Comprehensive costed risk models are maintained and frequently updated.

External Dependencies

1. Orders and contracts are 'casual' or ad hoc and are usually on suppliers' terms and conditions.

Purchases are often made by 'non-purchasing people' with few, if any, records of transactions made.

2. All suppliers are treated the same way, although some get more attention than others. Activity is 'today' orientated.

There is a legal basis for contracts placed.

3. Supply chains are generally understood and selective contracting strategies are used.

Few, if any, contract loopholes exist and supplier performance is monitored.

4. Key supply chains are understood in detail. Supplier relationships vary from 'arms-length' to 'close collaboration'.

    Vulnerability Analyses have been completed and contingency plans are in place.

5. An active and productive Supplier Relationship Management programme is in place. PRM is comprehensive.

Management Controls

1. Nothing is codified ... all decisions and actions are 'intuitive' and/or require top level approval.

2. Basic business standards, principles and policies are defined.

    A framework for Authority Delegation may exist but is most likely to be out of date.

3. As 2 but the policies and authorities are regularly reviewed and updated.

    Specific controls are defined which relate to the procurement process.

    Functional authorities are clearly specified (in terms of purpose and clarity).

4. As 3, plus authorities are substantial and reflect an empowered, skilful culture.

    Procurement emphasis is on acquiring best total return on acquisition costs.

5. As 4, plus procurement policies are all-embracing (i.e. they apply to all company personnel).

Market Conditions and Behaviours

1. The customer company (i.e. yours) generally feels helpless and is glad to get what they can.

2. The customer company is vulnerable to supplier sales tactics.

    Deals are the supplier's standard offering, but may be cosmetically enhanced to please the buyer.

3. Market distortions are understood and effectively counteracted.

   Fundamental drivers of supply costs are understood and trends are monitored.

4. Measures are in place which reflect awareness of the possibility of fraud and unprincipled supplier behaviour.

5. For key requirements, strategies are in place to influence supply markets and to elicit desired market responses (e.g. Reverse Marketing).

Handling the Unexpected

1. We know that the unexpected can happen but we hope that it won't.

2. 'Logical' contingency plans are in place but tend to be specific to a contract.

3. Comprehensive PRM is in place.

   By definition this includes strategies and contingency plans for all identified critical suppliers in terms of profit impact.

4. The company organisation exhibits the characteristics of High-Performing Teams and is agile yet goal-oriented when addressing unforeseen events.

   IT systems monitor numerous aspects of the supply chain over and above materials' flow. Examples are supplier solvency and natural catastrophe alerts relevant to the supply chain.

5. Not possible as no one can predict everything that might happen! The gap between '4' and '5' represents the space for the random event to materialise.

FURTHER QUESTIONS FOR URGENT ATTENTION

- How many of the undesirable events shown previously in Box 1 do we experience and what are we doing about them?

- Do we know which are our key supply chains and what potential events they are vulnerable to?

- Have we specifically evaluated how our corporate strategies and business plan can be helped or harmed by supply market events?

- Do we have a systematic process for identifying and evaluating procurement risks?

- Is our procurement process segmented into silos or does it lean more towards being a continuum of parallel operational and commercial activity?

② External Dependencies

A recent survey[1] reported that the main risk to supply chains was supplier failure, including an inability to obtain trade finance. This was highlighted by 75 per cent of respondents, followed by a physical incident impairing supplier facilities (43 per cent) and quality-failure leading to product recall or contamination (42 per cent).

The risk landscape of External Dependencies covers those situations where the customer company relies on suppliers to meet their obligations as set out in the purchase order or contract. It is important to distinguish between the physical means of supply (the 'supply chain') and the ability and commitment of the supply company to supply in the first place. Both aspects of External Dependency contain potential risks. The fact that piracy on the high seas and company financial failures are much in the news explains why this aspect of PRM receives almost exclusive attention on the business agenda. It is for this reason alone that this topic is the first to be addressed. However, this does not mean that issues such as Management Controls are less important. They

---

1   UK business magazine, *'CPO Agenda,'* Summer 2009.

too have the potential to destroy a company if lurking risks are allowed to materialise. But more of that in Chapter 5.

Examples of potential risk situations are:

- poor supplier performance;

- supplier pre-occupation with major projects or 'transformations';

- weak links in physical supply chains (inside and between supplier entities), losses and misdirections;

- damage to, and losses of, items still in the supply chain;

- false sense of security created by long term agreements;

- contract claims and penalties; under-compensation for losses;

- hostile supplier action and exploitative behaviour;

- over-assessment of importance of one's business to the supplier;

- over-dependence on too few sources;

- pushing suppliers too far;

- failure of outsourcing strategy;

- supplier bankruptcy;

- takeovers and mergers;

- exposure of unacceptable practices causing brand damage; regulatory interference;

- supplier fraud.

Each organisation must decide for itself how any of the potential risk situations previously listed would harm its operations but the fact that damage is done and that losses and costs are incurred is self-evident. It is important to be aware of the potential risks and the unlikely way in which some might materialise, and to do something about it.

RISKS AND REMEDIES

Poor supplier performance manifests itself in delayed or incorrect deliveries, shoddy work, additional costs and unsatisfied customers. There are a number of possible causes, even assuming that the supplier was properly assessed for capability in the first place. Problems often arise because quality or service specifications are ambiguous or incomplete. One company estimated that the problems of poor quality increased costs by 15 per cent so it is an area worth getting right ... and this analysis excluded the cost of customer dissatisfaction and such like. Commodity raw materials can be precisely specified but it is more difficult to do so for contract services. The job becomes easier if the overall notion of 'support service' is broken down into components such as response times; quality of technical help; service personnel continuity, and so on. Even a nebulous concept like a supplier's 'problem-solving capability' can be made more tangible with different levels of competence defined on a scale of '1' (very poor) to '10' (excellent). It is also tempting to think that performance requirements have been defined completely by, e.g. physically specifying a chemical or machined part. But performance issues such as delivery accuracy (quantity and time); flexibility to meet changed volume requirements; and speedy replacement of defective or damaged deliveries, etc, are just as important.

This last point raises the question 'what can we do to improve performance in future?' Some buyers feel that it is not their responsibility, but the supplier's, to do better. If this is a general policy then the company runs the risk of always having the handicap of inferior sources. The alternative policy is to say that, where appropriate, the company does wish its buyers to invest time with the supplier to improve things. If alternatives to the poor supplier are readily available then one would not necessary elect to do this. However, in other cases there could be a big payback, earning preferred-customer status from the supplier who has not just fixed the problems but moved on to achieve hitherto undreamt of capability and competitiveness. Sometimes a customer company has competences and resources that are not possessed by the supplier. Sharing these in a problem-solving way is proactive PRM at its best.

Poor performance can also arise because the supplier's eye is off the ball as a result of their *being preoccupied with major projects* (introducing new IT systems is a common culprit) or 'transformations' to change company culture. Checking out what big projects are planned is an important consideration before choosing which supplier is right to depend on at that time.

The key to fixing *weak links in physical supply chains* is to map the supply chain as a flow chart, if necessary going back beyond the supplier's supplier and right back to primary sources. Doing this is guaranteed to reveal facts, usually worrying ones, that were not previously known. Bringing these out into the open is itself a step towards more effective risk management. The next task is to imagine what things might go wrong along this flowchart and attach a probability to their happening. High, medium and low will suffice. Then assess their duration and impact on the business, if they occurred. This analysis reveals the top priorities for action.

Damage to, and losses of, items still in the supply chain would certainly be considered in the above analysis but there is another reason for singling it out. This has to do with who owns the items in question. If the contract is on a 'delivered' basis then the customer suffers only the cost of disrupting and rescheduling production and maybe also penalties for non-delivery imposed by the ultimate customer. This is bad enough, but it gets worse if ownership of the items took place ex-supplier and no indemnity actions were taken to insure against subsequent loss in transit. The insurance question also applies if the supply is on a delivered basis but the supplier organises a transport contractor to provide the logistics link.

A further risk is the *false sense of security created by long term agreements (LTAs)*. Typically these span a 1–3 year period; define commodity or performance specifications and provide agreed prices for different volumes that will possibly be purchased. LTAs may also state for how long prices will be kept stable, possibly include a price-review clause, and set out other terms and conditions. LTAs are useful as they save repeatedly having to re-negotiate terms and conditions. They also remove some uncertainty about the future and give suppliers enough confidence to book future supplies of raw materials. However, this does not guarantee supply security. It is dangerous to set up an LTA and then forget it.

Suppliers are not obliged to honour what they promise in LTAs. They are 'standing offers' and trade under their terms only becomes a legal commitment when purchase orders are placed. Although the latter are legally binding, they do not guarantee supply security. Suppliers can default on them or, at least, encounter problems which impair delivery performance. Critical supply arrangements therefore have to be managed in an ongoing way. This involves creating and sustaining appropriate supplier relationships. For items where there are several acceptable sources, then certainly establish LTAs in order to capture the operational benefits mentioned above. However, once an LTA is up and running with a preferred supplier, maintain contact with, and perhaps selectively use, other sources in order to play the market to ensure availability and cost competitiveness. In other cases, alternative sources may not be available or suppliers adopt unacceptable 'take-it-or-leave-it' stances on lead times and prices. In these circumstances, create Relationship Agreements (RAs) as the means of attracting lower initial prices and preferred treatment. The prime difference between an LTA and an RA is that the LTA locks supplier costs and performance into a 'quasi-contractual' box, whereas the RA creates the basis for transforming supply chain performance and cost effectiveness. Both cases require ongoing management of the buyer's relationship with the supplier, the greater effort with RAs being rewarded by bigger prizes.

Some suppliers and contractors use the tactic of bidding cheaply to win an order and then generate profit by placing *contract claims and penalties on their customers.* The target company is at risk to extra costs if unwarranted claims are in fact paid, with further costs arising if work or deliveries are stopped pending claims' resolution. There is nothing illegal about this and it might be argued that a buyer who leaves their company exposed to this tactic deserves it because they have not thought through things in advance. The key in all this is to establish beforehand a claims' handling process, although this does not remove the need to agree the job specification as clearly as possible before agreeing the contract.

The 'claims' handling process should distinguish between claims made as a result of changes, and claims arising from supplier hardship. The former may be due to extensions to the duration or scope of work required or even cancellation by the user. If, e.g. a claim for extra payment arose because the work was extended within the provisions of the contract, then this would be labelled an 'ordinary claim'. If the claim is outside the strict interpretation of the contract but it is deemed that local law would find that an obligation exists within the intent of the agreement, then this would be an 'extraordinary' claim. Finally a 'hardship' claim would be an extreme case which has no basis within the contract or in law. Normally there would be no obligation to settle it.

Wherever possible, deter frivolous claims by insisting on compliance with the original order and then attempt to resolve problems under normal contract procedures. Press the supplier to accept the results of risks he knowingly accepted at the time of commitment. Assess each claim on its own merits and, having checked any past precedents, aim for consistency in judging what response is appropriate, cost-justifying any proposed settlement. Avoid settling a claim solely to preserve goodwill. The authority to settle a claim should be held at the same level as the person authorised to commit the contract in the first place. I recall one very experienced project manager who had the authority to keep, and use, a company cheque book. He would negotiate a claim settlement hard but if it looked as though deadlock was on the cards he produced the chequebook and offered to settle for a small but credible amount there and then. The sight of money often stimulated immediate settlement and avoided the potentially far higher costs of prolonged further negotiations and possible litigation.

Tactical claiming is an example of where the customer company is exposed to calculated behaviour of a supplier as distinct from weaknesses or failures in the physical supply chain. *Hostile supplier action and exploitative behaviour* is another. Suppliers have long memories and understandably wait for opportunities for revenge against a customer against whom they hold a grudge ... maybe for past aggressive treatment when payments have been stopped or excessive price discounts demanded. Revenge is, of course, putting it dramatically and the salesperson will be skilled at turning the knife whilst still smiling at the customer! But business is business and if the seller feels he has an advantage *and* the buyer deserves it, then it will happen.

Hostile behaviour might take the form of cartel activity (see Chapter 3) or more usually appear as 'take it or leave it' price increase demands, if the customer is viewed as an exploitable proposition. Smart buyers put themselves in the supplier's shoes and see what their own company looks like from that viewpoint. The possibilities range from being an outright nuisance whom the supplier would like to lose, through to being a core customer critical to the supplier's future success. In between, the customer might be labelled 'exploitable' (that is, worth keeping so long as it keeps paying the high prices) or, much better, a development prospect where the supplier sees an attractive customer with whom they would like to do more business. Informed with this analysis the buyer can act accordingly, although it is easy to *over-assess the importance of one's business to the supplier.* The high risk scenario is to believe that the customer is always king and that suppliers should be grateful for the business they are given. Whilst some do fall into that category it is often the suppliers you really need who do not.

In their quest for volume-related cost reductions buyers rightly maximise their buying power by aggregating otherwise fragmented volumes and consolidating them on fewer suppliers. This can lead to *an over-dependence on too few sources*. The customer now heavily relies on the continued existence of the main supplier and simultaneously loses contact with alternatives. Any problem with that supplier will significantly disrupt the customer's business. Some customers have a rule which limits the amount of business they do with one supplier, defining this as a maximum percentage of the supplier's turnover that they will not exceed. A more strategic approach would be to keep an active second source in play whilst staying very close to the supplier with the majority of the business, taking regular updates of their business on top of the operational performance reviews already in place.

Another risk of placing too much business with any one supplier is that the drive for volume-related cost reductions eventually inflicts unbearable pain. *Pushing suppliers too far* can make the business unattractive for them. A major oil company had steadily placed more and more eggs in fewer supplier baskets without picking up signals that the supplier was approaching their pain threshold. This became apparent when the supplier, along with others acting apparently independently, refused to accept any more volume. In this case the remedy was a major change in the policy for managing supplier relationships, the aim being to collaborate more closely with key suppliers to tease out underlying wasted costs rather than simply pushing for price reduction by piling on more volume.

The 'outsourcing' label has certainly helped to increase CEO interest in procurement in recent years but the rush to capture cost reductions, or to follow fashion, means that the understanding of what makes outsourcing different from 'normal' procurement has been trodden underfoot. This, along with selecting the wrong outsourced partner, is what causes the *failure of an outsourcing strategy*. A person might seek cosmetic surgery to remove unwanted fat but if something else is removed which, after the event, proved to be rather more necessary than first thought, then it is rather too late to realise that the strategy was flawed in the first place. It is not new for buyers to address tactical 'make or buy' decisions, and to have the tools for doing it, but the outsourcing topic in its truest sense focuses on an activity or capability that is fundamental and core to the business. Deciding what is 'core' and 'non core' is still a challenge as it delves into the heart of what makes companies 'tick'. I asked one CEO how his company distinguished between the two. After some thought, and with an apologetic smile, he answered 'I guess a core activity is one that we haven't outsourced yet!' Another business pundit observed that 'medical research has enabled us to probe the deep secrets of life but we are not so well equipped to understand the deep secrets of corporate vitality.'

Choosing an outsourcing partner is the easier part of the challenge so long as the appraisal of alternatives goes much deeper than looking at capabilities and capacity. Success depends on what amounts to a process of courtship which reveals whether or not the two potential partners share the same business principles, values and strategic outlook. These cannot be determined by sending questionnaires as they have to be deduced over the course of many meetings where behaviours and attitudes can be judged. Deciding on the business case to outsource is more difficult and requires relentless logic, and CPOs are ideally positioned to provide leadership for the decision-making process. It divides into three parts: first, to examine the strategic importance to the business of the potentially outsourced activity; then to see if the supply market can provide a suitable outsource partner; then finally to examine the risks involved and how they might be mitigated. Of these three, it is again the first that requires deepest thought as it must judge issues such as how strongly the activity contributes to the strategic goals of the business; how capable and resourced the company is to do it as compared to others; and how fast the technology and knowledge needed to do it is changing and whether potential supply partners are better equipped to keep up with it and perhaps lead it. Even after the decision 'to outsource' has been made the new dependency can fail if relationships between supplier and customer are not nurtured and sustained.

Whilst a company rightly expects its buyers to win the best deals from their suppliers it is clearly unwise to exercise purchasing power to the extent that it causes *supplier bankruptcy*. Even if the existence of satisfactory alternatives ensures that supply is not disrupted the customer still runs the risk of sustaining reputational damage and loss of goodwill. Smart buyers therefore assess the supplier's ability to withstand pressure before applying more. This starts by checking if the supplier is already showing signs of company distress. Financial indicators, credit reports and city sentiment are three indicators of this. If the supplier passes this test then the buyer decides if they are equipped to push further and if contingency plans are ready should the supplier fight back or even withhold supplies.

Bankruptcy is not the only reason why sources disappear from supply chains. *Takeovers and mergers* have the same effect. Buyers can expect nasty surprises if they do not stay tuned in to company statements and the business press. This is an excellent reason to maintain dialogue with key sales contacts even in the good times. This contrasts with the many buyers who only have time to call in the salesperson when there are problems to complain about. After a takeover the 'new' owner or company will usually continue to offer the previous products or services but the risks come in the form of supply contracts being terminated in order to renegotiate tougher terms. Supply chain performance may also suffer because of operational preoccupation with merging the businesses or simply because the customer is now seen as less important than before. A previously good relationship with a key sales contact which can be sustained if he or she remains in position will play a big part in ensuring that supplies do not suffer at the hands of new company owners or cultures. More risks lurk if the new owner has financed the takeover by raising capital or borrowings. A once-viable source may now have the potential to show signs of financial distress if loan repayments become onerous.

We live in a glass-house world and the reputation of some companies has been damaged by the *exposure of unacceptable practices*. These are cases where it is not their own practices but those of others, sometimes far removed up the supply chain, which are deemed unacceptable. Familiar examples are the use of child labour; the exploitation of low paid workers labouring in sweat-shop conditions, and the unsustainable use of scarce natural resources. The consequence is damage to company reputation and to suffer close scrutiny, and maybe restraint, from regulators and lobby groups. A customer company cannot be held responsible for everyone else in the supply universe but the world of public relations works on emotion and not logic. It is realistic to expect a company to define its requirements for responsible principled behaviour from its immediate and next tier suppliers, and to assist and audit as appropriate. Their own behaviours must also match these ideals. All this should be accompanied by an ongoing public relations process that sustains the positive news in the good times and mobilises damage limitation in the bad. Without media training, board members and senior company managers will be like lambs slaughtered by the Press.

Supplier fraud is an issue with ramifications in two areas: External Dependencies and Management Controls. Whilst the majority of suppliers will be tough but still behave honestly, buyers are at risk if they assume that all of them are above reproach. Normal contractual terms provide some protection or redress but risks remain if other checks and balances are absent. Internal procedures must insure against accepting and paying for deliberate over-supply of goods or services, or higher-than-agreed unit prices being assigned to correct volumes. Inflation of sub-contractor invoices is another way for the main contractor to overcharge an unsuspecting customer. Fraud can also be perpetrated at the pre-award stage of the procurement process by suppliers who interfere with bid invitation and evaluation processes. Such risks will be minimised if the buyer is consistent and firm in applying clear procedures which ensure transparency and even-handedness; which provide audit trails, and which define the steps to be taken if corruption of the bidding process is detected.

PRINCIPLES AND RISK PREVENTION

The above is not an exhaustive list of potential risks but gives a fair indication of their widespread nature. Although examples of preventative measures are given it is better to create a risk management process that works out its own solutions in the first-place. Anything less will be 'doing PRM by numbers' and is merely selecting a risk management tactic from a menu of possibly inappropriate solutions.

Traditional buyers are typically focused on the deals they have made and know them inside out. But this is only part of the story. Effective PRM of External Dependencies requires deep understanding of the steps in the physical supply chain; of the supply company at the end of it, and the individual who represents that company as a customer account manager. Once the supply chain is mapped as a flow chart it is easier to conduct a vulnerability analysis, although this requires some creativity in imagining what disruptive events might occur at each link in the chain. Do not dismiss events that are deemed unlikely but simply assign a low, medium or high probability to them. Next, assess the possible duration of each event and also its likely impact on the business. This analysis will quickly reveal what the main risks are, to which the solutions are often self-evident.

Now consider the supply company and what is known about them. Are they strategic or not? A strategic supplier is one whose presence and performance is key to achieving the customer company's business goals. In most cases there will be significant annual expenditures with them and few, if any, acceptable alternative sources. The relationship with them will be long rather than short term and will require ongoing involvement by senior-level management on both sides. What is known about their business strategy; their financial viability; their investment plans; their business continuity plans, and so on? How good is their procurement process? If it is inferior to the customer's then the prices paid are rewarding them for inefficiency. Crucially, how do they view the customer? To be labelled a nuisance or exploitable customer is bad news. Obviously it is better to be seen as a development prospect or a customer who is core to their business success. Companies who have a strategic view of procurement, set out to influence these considerations and create the supply markets they need rather than just accept the way they are. This includes holding suppliers accountable to perform in line with the promises they made when they won the order. Personal relationships are important and the buyer should know as much as they can about the supplier's representative. What motivates them? Who do they report to? Do they have the authority to agree with what the buyer wants? What can be found out from them about their pricing policy and how costs build up in their internal supply chain?

The key message is the importance of analysis and the likelihood that this will reveal powerful and usable facts not known hitherto. It can be difficult to find time to invest in up-front risk identification and assessment but it is better to spend this time now rather than to have it hijacked by an unforeseen disruption. Information is power but it does not fall into a buyer's lap. They have to searched for it. As one CPO said when faced with an apparently insoluble supply problem 'the deeper I dig the luckier I get' in finding the key to its solution.

FURTHER QUESTIONS FOR URGENT ATTENTION

- Do we distinguish between strategic suppliers and those who are not critical? Are they treated differently?

- Do we have flow charts for our critical supply chains and have we located the weakest links?

- How do we assess supplier performance and do any of our strategic suppliers show signs of financial distress?

- How do suppliers assess our performance? Would we be considered their best customer?

- If one of our suppliers develops a cost or quality innovation, would we be the first customer they call?

3 Market Conditions and Behaviours

In January 2005 the European Union lifted restrictions on textile imports from China. This was the precursor for what became known as Bra Wars.[1] Why? Because European retailers hired Chinese manufacturers to make clothes at dramatically reduced costs. Import quotas were then hastily re-introduced in August of that year to protect the continent from the deluge of Chinese goods. A huge volume of garments were thus held in limbo in the supply chain: 48 million sweaters; 17 million pairs of men's trousers; four million T-shirts, and three million bras to be precise.

More recently it was announced that England will see four new football stadiums built before or just after the 2012 Olympics.[2] The commentator questions whether the football clubs concerned will have problems finding suitable contractors to

---

1   *The Independent*, 27 August 2005, 'Revealed: How Bra Wars devastate the world's poor'.
2   Building.co.uk, 24 August 2007, 'Stadium overload'.

take on these projects in an already busy market. Even if they do not, there is the distinct possibility that costs will escalate as supply struggles to keep up with demand. Further, tender prices are forecast to rise by 34 per cent over a five year period with the Olympics work being one of the main causes.

These are examples of big issues that affect a whole supply market sector rather than a particular supply chain and the vulnerable links in it. 'Market Conditions and Behaviours' therefore refers to the supply market environment with which the company interacts via its procurement process before and after contract commitment. Here the supply market is viewed as a whole as distinct from focusing on individual suppliers and supply chains as in External Dependencies. Specific issues are the composition of the market, its capacity and the way it behaves. Composition deals with the number of sources available; how individual companies are owned and perhaps related; and emergent or declining technologies. Market capacity refers to the volumes available and whether demand is chasing supply or vice versa. The popular terms buyers' or sellers' markets apply here. Available capacity will wax and wane in sympathy with economic cycles but there will also be demand spikes which temporarily distort the market. Market behaviour will be governed by economic influences, such as what are the main cost drivers at work and what pricing policies are in play at different stages of product life cycles. Whilst some markets behave in a competitive way and follow shifts in supply and demand, other markets behave in the way that suppliers decide they should. Cartels are a case in point. To assume that all markets are competitive and that all prices are calculated by cost-plus logic is to run the biggest risk of all ... that one's input prices, and hence margins and budget utilisation, are effectively set where the suppliers want them to be. The big question then is 'who exactly is running our business?!'

Examples of potential risk situations are:

- price and supply volatility;

- upward price pressures;

- lack of early warning of price and capacity changes;

- supply shortages due to competitor demands, global events or natural disasters;

- loss of competitive sources because of mergers and acquisitions;

- over-eagerness to source in Low Cost Countries;

- unexpected changes to regulations;

- unfavourable currency movements;

- being held hostage to monopolies;

- being targeted by supplier cartels;

- invoicing scams;

- information brokering;

- disrupted e-Auctions.

RISKS AND REMEDIES

Price and supply volatility are the enemy of smoothly planned cash flow and production schedules. Attempting to follow constant fluctuations carries the risk of adding to costs as well as consuming time that could otherwise be spent on proactive rather than reactive work. Some companies peg their purchase prices for commodity raw materials to indices which are published monthly. This has advantages in some circumstances and if it is wished to continue with this approach then it is worth negotiating with the supplier to introduce some stability by changing prices every three months or more instead of monthly. Make sure that only that part of total price which is exposed to, say, feedstock costs is changed and not total cost. There is no reason why a supplier's overheads or labour costs should change monthly but the supplier wins if these components can also be increased stealthily by burying them in total cost. These comments are only the tip of the 'understanding price' iceberg and companies are well advised to give their buyers time to probe and understanding supplier costs and how these and other factors affect prices. Formulating internal cost targets and working with, and persuading, the supplier to meet them is much more strategic than simply seeing what prices the market is offering and negotiating a discount. Strategic work then extends to setting up price agreements with the supplier which fix prices for a year or more, whilst also agreeing the process to be used when it is time for price review.

Agreeing a fixed price contract moves some of the price-uncertainty risk to the supplier. Although the buyer may effectively pay for this through higher prices in the short term the benefit of price-certainty has other advantages. The CEO of a company supplying to an aircraft manufacturer agreed a 3-year fixed price supply deal which mirrored a 3-year agreement he had negotiated with the customer. He could thus be certain of margins for the contract term which in turn allowed smoother financial planning for the duration.

Joint forward planning with the supplier also helps smooth out supply fluctuations. Sharing forecast business schedules is a start. If a long term agreement is in place to give the supplier some confidence of future needs then they can make choices about producing ahead of scheduled requirements. Building stock levels to provide surge capacity and flatten demand spikes is anathema to those of the lean production school. But the result is a win-win if this allows the supplier to optimise their production costs, and if deliveries are made on a consignment stock basis. Here the customer does not pay for supplies when they are delivered but when they are used. Buyers risk sub-optimal solutions if they try to solve these problems by themselves.

Upwards price pressure is always quicker to make its presence felt than downwards! Again it is hard-earned sales revenue or budgeted monies that are at risk if buyers allow markets to dictate prices rather than aiming to exert some control on them by setting their own targets; having price stability and price review mechanisms in place; and being prepared with counter arguments to repel attacks. One measure of the extent to which a customer is regarded as an easy target is the quality of the price-increase argument put forward by the salesperson. Generally these are flimsy and usually cite rises in some commodity prices (e.g. crude oil) as the reason. The request must be firmly rejected if the seller has no further ammunition to withstand detailed probing, and if it is clear that they are doing little themselves to manage cost increases. The risk then is that the seller adopts a 'take it or leave it' stance, in which case the trained buyer will switch to alternative negotiating tactics focusing on the bigger picture of the value of doing business together and the particular benefits of the customer 'as a customer'. Market movements are not the only reason for price increases. Crafty sellers use a number of tactics, mostly legal, to increase prices by stealth. The customer is at risk of paying these if their systems and business review routines do not detect them and if the buyer has not been trained to spot them in the first place.

As a minimum, *lack of early warning of price and capacity changes* adds to costs because operating and financial plans are disrupted. The added risk is defaulting on customer commitments because supplies are not available. Whilst it might be possible to mitigate some of the uncertainty by building stability and availability clauses into a contract, it is better to get ahead of the game and understand what drives changes in the first place. The choice is between understanding how markets work and calling supplies from them as appropriate, as distinct from letting market movements happen and trying to insulate one's company from their effects.

Whilst many market movements will be linked to the economic cycle *additional supply shortages will arise from spikes in competitor demands, global events or natural disasters.* To some extent these can be predicted or at least their possibility recognised and discussed with key sources. Establish what a key supplier's own procurement strategy is for the resources or commodities concerned and tap into their own analysis of what drives their own supply chains. If they have done good work then the buyer can learn from it. If they have not, then buyers have a negotiating advantage when suppliers plead hardship. Also, find out how they analyse trends in their customer markets, as this might highlight other events which will affect supply availability. Building Olympic stadia, athletes' villages and transport infrastructures all have a massive impact on local supply capacity but are foreseeable market events. An American presidential election, and the build up to it, is said to make a huge drain on the raw materials for paper products. Refurbishment of the local branch of a national store chain will make large but temporary calls on a whole range of local contractors. Likewise preparations for the Ryder Cup, once its next venue has been announced. Less easy to predict, but still potentially disruptive, are company promotions. An oil company's campaign to boost gasoline sales by giving away classy glassware made a big dent in European bottle-making capacity and made life difficult for those in the drinks business. The biggest risk is to assume that once a contract has been set up then it can look after itself. If the supply relationship is important then there is no alternative but to nurture it and maintain constant dialogue with supply contacts as well as monitoring the key indicators and predictors of market behaviour and, not least, the weather.

Loss of competitive sources because of mergers and acquisitions has already been identified in Chapter 2 as a possible risk but it is addressed again here for another reason. Whilst the previous concern was to do with an existing supply company being taken over, further risks arise if PRM does not also survey those whole sectors of the supply market which city analysts see as ripe for consolidation. One prerequisite for successful PRM is that it is whole supply market sectors, relevant to the business, which are kept under a 'world watch' as distinct from merely keeping up to date with the status of specific supply contracts and the parties with whom they have been agreed.

Shrinking or expensive local supply markets might drive the buyer to be *over-eager to source from Low Cost Countries*. The cost advantages are usually very apparent but the risks less so. These include the creation of longer vulnerable supply chains; exposure to import protocols; start-up problems and quality issues. The latter are often exacerbated by the fact that the main source is a front for a network of sub-suppliers behind the scenes. A less obvious risk arises by leaving domestic suppliers out of the equation. This manifests itself tactically and strategically. Tactically means underestimating the total costs of bringing in the 'new' source whilst also failing to assess the potential for cost-reduction/performance-improvement domestically. The combined effect is an unrealistically inflated cost incentive for going offshore. Strategically it means overly concentrating on qualifying the new source and setting up the deal whilst failing to plan how the whole market (that is, offshore and domestic) will be played. The outcome might be that there is no domestic fall back should this be needed. Too often, going offshore is a reaction to poor domestic supply performance rather than a step in a larger strategy to create high-performing sources at home. The strategic way means that the buyer is always on the case and managing ongoing relationships. However, this is rare as it is more usual for a new deal to be set up and then left to run itself.

The Bra Wars reference earlier provides ample evidence of the mayhem caused by *unexpected changes in regulations*. Although perhaps less unexpected, the impact of the USA's 'Buy American' policy will create dilemmas for buyers in US Government Departments whose use of potentially better-value-for-money sources (e.g. Canadian) will be curtailed.[3] Where it is sufficiently important to do so, a company can stay tuned to, and possibly influence, legislative trends via relevant trade associations or by direct approaches, if big

---

3   *Supply Management*, 25 June 2009, 'Canada fears US protectionism'.

enough. It is also important to differentiate between import protocols, which may remain fairly static, and volume quotas which may be more variable. As a minimum the knowledge that a supply chain's operation depends on trouble-free import processes will heighten awareness of the need to monitor the regulatory scene. A company including this in its ongoing PRM process will be better equipped to handle changed rules than a competitor who does not.

Unfavourable currency movements are an ever-present risk where overseas procurement is concerned. A number of financial instruments are available to offset risks in this area and a company's CFO will be well-versed in them. An additional risk is that an overseas supplier may be reluctant to sell into the customer's domestic market because of unfavourable exchange-rate implications. This can limit the customer's choice for suppliers of key resources and result in an uncomfortable dependence on one, or too few, local sources. One option is to purchase using foreign rather than local currency, thus removing the Forex hurdle for the foreign source. If this stimulates competition then the decision depends on the arithmetic of keener prices offsetting the costs of using foreign currency. Another incentive may be the desire to increase the capacity and maybe security of the supply chain by being able to access alternatives. If the buyer thinks only in terms of 'we only have one source' then that is the way it will remain. If instead they ask 'what barriers do we have to remove to create more sources' then the mind is open to creative alternatives which, if feasible, reduce risk

The risk of *being held hostage to monopolies* is the buyer's nightmare scenario notwithstanding the fact that the monopoly supplier is viable and not heading for bankruptcy. A monopolistic situation exists where there is only one supplier available in the supply market capable of meeting customer requirements. This is not healthy and the risks are: vulnerability to stopped supply; prices significantly higher than competitive levels; an arrogant stance by the salesperson, and problems with quality and general performance. Sometimes the monopoly problem is of the customer's own making because specifications are too specific to one supplier and perfectly acceptable alternatives are excluded. Or, other possible suppliers do exist but are rejected because of past problems with poor quality. Buyers leave their company at risk if all they do is accept what the markets offer and flip flop between whoever is offering best prices or posing fewest problems.

The first step in reducing monopoly risk is to challenge the requirements that exclude other sources from meeting them. Early involvement is key. Make sure that the buyer works closely with the designers to design out difficult supply situations wherever practical. The next is to see if other sources can be developed to provide some competition. A thorough market analysis is required: locally, regionally and globally. There are many local and regional monopolies, but few truly global ones. If the search does not come up with an immediate alternative it may reveal the possibility of developing one. A chemical company suffered badly by having only one haulage contractor to provide road-tanker haulage for its liquid products. Every aspect of supplier performance was below par. A procurement colleague noticed that there was another haulage company in the region but whose capability, albeit first class, was restricted to powdered cargoes. This company was persuaded to diversify into liquid products as well. Their initial doubts about being able to do so were allayed by the customer company loaning them technical and project experts to help them make the transition. Some, but not all, of the business was given to the new company. The incumbent company's loss of volume provided the spur to shake off complacency and work with the customer company to improve performance. The buyer can now access two competitive sources of comparable capability, and continues to use both in order to keep it that way. The reactive buyer would have ditched the old and gone with the new and the pendulum would have continued to swing between one monopoly and another.

Sometimes though, there really is no other choice and one has to do one's best with the monopoly. Most people perceive a monopoly to be in a strong position simply because they have the ability to control the market. That premise must be challenged and the best way to do this is to search for a weakness and thus change the balance of power. A weakness may be that the monopoly is crucially dependent on the customer for some reason, or a practice may be exposed which has the potential to embarrass them publicly. Arguing them down on price will be fruitless. However, there are many components to a deal and it is possible to win concessions from the strong supplier which are not as visible as price and hence easier to agree to. These are still valuable to the buyer, but whilst this lessens the pain of having to pay the asking price, it is not enough. The buyer must maintain constant contact with the supplier and regard them as an extension of their own business, staying concerned about total business status and outlook over and above product or service performance. Build a direct relationship with the sales person and increase understanding about what their ambitions are and what they have to achieve to satisfy themselves and those to whom they report. This work may need to be done at a senior level. Monopoly suppliers typically build strong customer relationships at board level as part of their plan to sustain the belief that the monopoly supplier is the only acceptable game in town.

The buyer who is not streetwise and who is shackled to seeking three bids every time a contract is in the offing is at risk of *being targeted by supplier cartels*. These are illegal but, despite some high profile and expensive court judgements against them, they still exist in certain supply market sectors. Suppliers collude with each other to decide who should win the business on offer and all, except the one chosen to succeed this time around, will submit high bids designed not to win the business. Competitive forces are not driving prices down and so the buyer will pay much more than if it they were. 100 per cent mark-ups have been known, with company profit or budgets being the direct casualties. These are the consequences if the buyer wrongly assumes that the market is competitive and approaches it accordingly (that is, by seeking bids). Even if this happens it is not too late for the skilled buyer to pick up the symptoms of cartel operation, to call off the bidding exercise, and then deal with suppliers one-by-one in such a way that they are confused about the buyer's intentions. Uncertainty and doubt stops cartels being triggered.

Whilst they may not be major risks, *invoicing scams* can be minor irritants albeit still exposing the victim to financial loss. For example, companies are often invited to be included in a trade directory, apparently for no charge. The reality is that there *is* a cost which is usually extortionate, but this fact is hidden away in the small print of the agreement. Falsification and alteration of sub-contract invoices are further manifestations of corrupt market behaviour, discussed in Chapter 2 in connection with supplier fraud. One supplier salesman was particularly brazen in asking a senior buyer to 'sign for some samples'. The latter's scepticism was dispelled when the salesperson mentioned that 'X', a colleague of the buyer in another department, had already agreed in principle (see Chapter 4 and 'breach of confidentiality'). The buyer signed, but it then turned out that his signature was used falsely to purchase a shipment of the product rather than to receive free samples. One will always marvel at the ingenuity of those with criminal tendencies and there can be no absolute safeguard against their activities other than to know that such things happen and, rather than listen to the plausible 'sales-pitch', to pay more attention to the tiny voice of doubt and probe relentlessly until it is silenced.

Information brokering is another manifestation of corrupted market behaviour. The culprit will be a supply company who knows that a customer is coming to the market to invite bids or tenders. However, the supplier is not interested in winning the business. By dubious means, and not always with the help of a buyer who is selling secrets, they will establish what level of bid will win the business. They then sell that information to a supplier who does want the business. If necessary the tendering process is then manipulated so that the supplier who has bought the information wins the order. A buyer who is naïve and whose company does not have, and adhere to, a robust tendering process is exposed to these antics where others will gain at the buyer's expense.

Widespread use of the internet has made it easier for suppliers and customers to talk to each other, thus providing buyers with new ways of inviting and identifying best bids from suppliers in competitive markets. However, if the buyer is not aware of what can go wrong then their attempts to get best value for money is exposed to *disrupted e-auctions*. The process can be flawed from the start if the buyer has not been sufficiently clear in specifying their need, and then the process itself can deter some suppliers from bidding and thus artificially limit the buyer's choice of possible sources. Reasons for not wishing to participate include previous bad experiences and the suppliers' often justifiable concern that the process commoditises what they offer. This over-focus on price destroys relationships. Disinterested suppliers can disrupt the process by offering a very low price at the start of the auction (thereby deterring others from bidding); by submitting late bids, or not participating at all. The answer is to be very selective about when to use this so-called 'reverse auction' technique and to handle it with all the consistency and integrity that would accompany a traditional tendering process. Avoid being predictable by limiting its use to occasional market testing and to capturing one-off savings.

PRINCIPLES AND RISK PREVENTION

The previous section shows the diverse ways in which supply market behaviours can make life difficult for the buyer, and gives examples of what buyers can do to ease the pain. It is not possible to prepare responses for all eventualities, neither is this desirable since all they will do is deal with the symptoms rather than the causes of problems. The underlying issue is that buyers often do not have strategies for exerting (at least some) control in their supply markets. Risk events are therefore reacted to rather than mitigated.

The guiding principle is that the buyer should develop and change supply markets to suit the needs of their business rather than to compromise that need by accepting markets as they are. This needs a strategy, which is a plan to ensure that a situation that the company desires is in fact achieved. To qualify for the strategy label the desired situation will be one that does not exist today and will not occur without the company's efforts to bring it into being. Further, the company's ambitions and/or viability will be damaged if the goal is not achieved.

Too many procurement teams are rendered helpless by an unexpected supply-related event, not quite knowing how to respond to it. A strategy, with contingency plans, reduces this risk. They do not have to be cumbersome to be useful. One manufacturing company's procurement team was doing a good 'today' job of creating and managing supply contracts; optimising total costs within the scope of the contracts; operating supply chains, and dealing with issues as they arose. However, it was difficult to discern a 'buying game plan' in terms of how it was decided which suppliers got what business, and how foreseeable market changes were going to be addressed. The solution was to lay out a simple plan for each critical item purchased (mainly raw materials) which addressed these questions:

- What are the available sources?

- What volume is forecast to be purchased from each source for the current year?

- What will this cost?

- What volumes will be required next year and what will be the cost targets?

- How will this total volume be split amongst the sources?

- What are the objectives in doing this?

- What key actions are now needed?

The four priorities taken into account were: price stability and predictability; supply chain security; sources and availability, and cost levels.

Strategic Procurement means managing suppliers and influencing supply markets so that they respond, now and in future, in the way the company needs them to in order to succeed in achieving its objectives. The underlying belief is that supply markets can be changed and not merely accepted as is. Strategies are developed via a collaborative cross-functional process within the company which not only engages talent and knowledge in strategy preparation but also leads to co-ordinated commercially aware behaviours. All this sounds ambitious but it is eminently practical once a company focuses its intellect on developing a strategy and then channels its energy in that direction. This is very different from what most companies do which is to think only in terms of short-term muscle power and 'piling higher, buying cheaper'.

FURTHER QUESTIONS FOR URGENT ATTENTION

- What local, national or global events are scheduled in the next four years which may temporarily drain supply resources which are vital for our business?

- Do we have the best suppliers in the industry as our partners?

- How are we leveraging our company's size in our partnerships with our suppliers?

- Do we have reason to be suspicious that supplier cartels are operating against us? Have suppliers declined to bid without good reason, or tried to influence our bidding processes?

- Do we have a process for developing a procurement strategy and, if so, what does the end product look like?

(4) Procurement Process

The recent past has not been an unqualified success for those in the vanguard of procurement change. A popular view of procurement is that it should get on with the simple job of delivering savings and try not to wreck things. One Supply Management roundtable discussion was admirably self-critical in acknowledging that procurement is having a tough time getting its message across.[1] And these were high-impact CPOs speaking, not lowly buyers. In late 2007, McKinsey reported that companies have failed to explore the full potential of procurement with a lack of talent, aspiration and corporate alignment hampering its impact.[2] Elsewhere, a leading figure in international procurement proclaimed, 'Purchasers must change. If they don't then the work will be done by lawyers and bankers.'

Tragically the issue is not just about procurement's image and whether or not it sits at the top table. Lives are at risk as well. The sharp rise in deaths of British soldiers serving in overseas war zones has called into question the government's procurement

---

1   *Supply Management*, 20 September 2007, 'Profession must sell itself'.
2   *Supply Management*, 29 November 2007, 'Call for buyers to realise potential'.

of eight helicopters.[3] A Public Accounts Committee report slammed the project, describing it as a 'gold standard cock-up'. It was discovered that software problems prevented the helicopters from flying unless the sky was cloudless and landmarks clearly visible. Longer ago it was the same story at local level when a county council purchased a mobile library which was so heavily accessorised that it could not carry any books without exceeding weight limits.

Why is procurement failing to shine as brightly as it has the potential to? One reason is that its role is seldom associated with the goals of the business but is, instead, preoccupied with cost reduction. The self-harming paradox is that many senior procurement people define their importance by the vast amount of money they spend, and then pin their ambitions on making it as small as possible. There is little credibility in a business process seemingly bent upon cost-saving itself out of existence.[4]

'Procurement Process' covers all activities from deciding on a business need to committing to a supplier to satisfy that need, and ensuring that the outcome is acceptable. This definition includes the information systems and decision-making tools which support the process if it is to be well-informed and effective. The key stages are specifying the need; searching the market and soliciting offers from suppliers; negotiating and awarding the contract, and finally keeping a commercial watch on overall contract performance.

So what can go wrong? Examples of potential risk situations are:

---

3   *Supply Management*, 23 July 2009.
4   *CPO Agenda*, Spring 2008, Vol. 4 No. 1, Cover Feature, 'At the helm or all at sea?' R.C. Russill.

- release of information which reduces negotiating power;

- commercially unaware behaviour (buying signals, sales tactics);

- poor specifications;

- insufficient standardisation;

- no early procurement involvement (specifications, alternatives, funding);

- 'make' versus 'buy' not considered;

- wrong assessment of potential supplier's suitability;

- flawed contract strategy with potential contract loopholes;

- inappropriate 'market approach tactics';

- corrupted bid responses and tender evaluation;

- insufficient use of potential negotiating power;

- over-focus on price and inadequate assessment of total cost of ownership;

- 'soft money' ignored;

- inappropriate or poor Supplier Relationship Management;

- asset disposal mishandled;

- insufficient market analysis of competitive dynamics, capacities, cost drivers;

- under-trained personnel.

RISKS AND REMEDIES

Procurement activity is often depicted as a sequential process which reflects the different decisions made by different people with different authorities. In the first place the budget holder, or user, decides what is needed and has the requisitioning authority to decide how much money will be allocated to meet the business need. Then it is over to procurement to find the best source and to place an order or contract. Obviously only suppliers who can meet the specified need will be in contention, and the 'best' of them will be the source who offers the best price and delivery time. In some circumstances the business may be split between two or more suppliers. With the contract in their pocket the supplier gets down to business, eventually completes the assignment, and is paid.

Streetwise sales personnel like this partitioned situation as they know that, initially, they may be talking to budget holders who are not commercially aware. Often these are knowledge specialists like engineers and technical folk who live in a black and white world. They are trained to get the facts right, to deal in logic, and to answer accurately any questions put to them. So if the salesperson asks what the budget is for a potential purchase, they get a precise answer that is commercially useful to them. I know, because, as a chemical engineer and budget holder, I've been there! The budget-holder's *release of this and similar information reduces negotiating power.* The seller now has an idea of what the customer is expecting to pay and will price their offer accordingly. It is an unequal contest. The user is working on the basis that prices are based on costs, whilst the seller is aiming for the price they think they can get. And so the buyer pays more than is necessary. This risk is greatly reduced if the user is briefed about these different pricing approaches, and is also equipped with the politician's skill of dealing with questions. So now, on being asked what the budget is, they come back with another question: 'Why do you ask? Are you afraid of not winning the order? What price do you think you'll have to offer to be certain of winning it?' And so on.

A commercial-awareness briefing of users also reduces the risk of *commercially unaware behaviour*. Sellers are trained to pick up buying signals. When they hear a customer say 'your product is better than anything else' or 'you are the only people we can depend on to do a good job' ... then they know that they have little or no competition for the order and increase price accordingly. Sales tactics are also a revelation to non-sellers. Advise users that they are being targeted; that buyers are often avoided until the user has been 'sold' on the seller's offering so that the buyer is presented with a fait accompli; and that aggressive closing tactics can force a decision before the user is really ready to commit to it.

Poor specifications are a major source of financial exposure, and mean that the buyer either pays too much or does not get what is really needed. Typically, a customer tells the supplier what they wish to purchase rather than explaining the need that is to be satisfied. A drinks company specified a sugar product for its fruit juices. The sugar was in short supply and was priced high accordingly. The customer then realised that the business need was for sweetening, not sugar. This opened the door to alternative products which satisfied the need, were in plentiful supply, and cost 30 per cent less than sugar. Costly variations on the specifications' theme include slight but unnecessary differences in quality, or features which merely reflect user preference and do not fundamentally affect fitness for purpose. One food company was buying 37 different types of chicken flavouring until it realised the high costs of doing so. *Insufficient standardisation* such as this leads to higher unit prices for smaller order quantities plus extra inventory costs. 'We are experts in variety!' said their self-critical CPO.

'*No early involvement*' is the buyer's common complaint, but it is a two-edged sword. Its advantage is that users and others can be briefed on commercial awareness and sales tactics. Users can also be enlisted to ferret out information from suppliers who will tell things to customer technical specialists that they will not divulge to buyers. Such information obtained during early technical discussions comes in useful during later negotiations, but only if the buyer has acquired it via early involvement. However, things can go wrong if the buyer is perceived to be playing a negative or policing role. Questioning a chosen specification or a preferred supplier is fine if the buyer can do it in a positive 'this might help you' way, but the barriers come down if the user thinks the buyer is telling them how to do their job. Early involvement also highlights the risks of developing a specification which is unique to the firm concerned and can only be supplied from the one source willing and able to match it. Self-imposed monopoly supply situations arise in this way.

Some longstanding but now obscure research looked at the potential savings on product cost that arose depending on when procurement considerations were first taken into account in the product development process. Procurement involvement at concept stage correlated with a 75 per cent potential cost saving; leaving it until the development stage reduced this to 12 per cent, and presenting buyers with a fait accompli at production time left them with only a 5 per cent savings' potential. Early involvement also curtails the tendency always to 'buy new' when re-using already-owned assets would work just as well.

Admittedly *'make v buy'* considerations will not apply for many things that a company buys (e.g. raw materials) but there will be occasions when risks arise if the options are neither considered nor fully thought through. For example, outsourcing a data-processing operation may make headcount sense but raises the spectre of lost competitive advantage if commercially sensitive data leaks out. Sub-contracting engineering work may be one way of handling more business when one's own machining capacity is fully stretched but may not necessarily be the correct strategy all the time. One company set up several machining sub-contracts but experienced higher costs simply because each contractor was having to purchase steel in the smaller batches commensurate with their part of the total workload. The solution was for the customer to set up a steel supply contract which covered its total volume requirement and then instructed the sub-contractors to buy the steel on these terms. Another route would be for the customer to purchase steel and issue it 'free' to the contractors ... a perfectly valid option but one that creates the new risks of misappropriation or waste. These can be managed providing they are recognised beforehand.

Traditionally, supplier appraisal involved being sure that the product sold met the required specifications and that the supplier was financially viable. Nowadays much more is required and there is, consequently, the heightened risk of *wrongly assessing a potential supplier's suitability*. Product or service suitability and financial soundness are simply the start points, although the latter can be an ongoing concern given that the current economic climate has increased the number of suppliers heading for bankruptcy.[5] Good supplier appraisal has to include what it will be like to work with, and be seen to be working with, the company concerned. This is over and above their being able to satisfy product specifications. This is illustrated by a US manufacturing company's assessment of the following aspects of supplier performance which were particularly important to them as they searched for an alternative supplier to replace, partially, an unacceptable incumbent:

- delivery accuracy (timing and quantity);

- responsiveness to variations in order-quantity;

- inter-company communication and EDI capability;

- cost levels;

- cost management;

- problem solving capability;

- willingness to collaborate on innovations.

---

5   See Chapter 7 for a list of signs that indicate when a supplier might be in financial distress. The list is given as an example of external supply chain indicators which, so long as they are kept under scrutiny, provide early warnings of disruptive events.

The appraisal checklist becomes more searching if the customer is looking for a 'partnership' relationship with a supplier and will include issues such as compatible values and complementary strategic intent.

The risks of *flawed contract strategy with potential contract loopholes* range from wasted time and costs arising from ill-defined contractual requirements through to being vulnerable to contractor fraud. This is expanded in the chapter on Market Conditions and Behaviours but the topic is mentioned now simply to emphasise that developing a robust contract strategy is a vital aspect of the procurement process.

All the good work arising from early involvement; producing legitimate needs-oriented specifications, and being commercially smart will be undone if the supply market is approached in the wrong way to invite offers. *Inappropriate 'market approach tactics'* include inviting three bids when cartels exist; soliciting other offers when there is an overwhelming case to extend a contract newly awarded to an existing supplier; insisting on formal tendering when the need is unclear and can only be clarified through early discussions with a supplier, and seeking competitive prices for low-value orders. All these carry the risk of wasting time and costs or paying sky-high prices. The problem is that buyers are often instructed to follow procedures that are internally focused and do not reflect how supply markets work in real life. A chess master will use a variety of opening moves in order to keep the other player guessing. The buyer should do likewise and be able to choose whether to open the 'game' by seeking tenders; seeking bids (initial offers); engaging in parallel or single negotiations; or simply not searching the market at all for competitive offers if they believe that a recently-used supplier's prices are still competitive. Buyers need the authority to be flexible. If they are not, the supplier will anticipate the opening moves and will price accordingly.

The process used to invite and develop offers from suppliers can range from the informal discussions through to formal tendering. Each has merit if the right horse is put on the right course. Tendering carries additional and particular requirements that the process and timetable is strictly adhered to and that bid evaluation is conducted in a transparently fair way so that no one supplier obtains an advantage. If the buyer departs from these strictures, e.g. by giving one supplier more time than the others to submit a bid, then the impartiality of the process is compromised. An unsuccessful supplier recently used the claim of *corrupted tender evaluation* to win a court case against a potential customer company who placed their business elsewhere. In this case the word 'corrupted' is used to describe a faulty process. However, tendering processes can be impaired by corrupt behaviour on both sides of the table. For buyer transgressions see the chapter on Management Controls, whilst the chapter on Market Behaviour addresses what suppliers can get up to.

Most people believe that they are natural negotiators, and indeed this was so when they were young children. This belief stays with them as they grow older, but educational themes and life experience can subtly reduce actual effectiveness, leading to *insufficient use of potential negotiating power*. The risks to the buyer's organisation are that money is left on the table and that less than desirable outcomes are accepted. Training can partially redeem matters by helping participants to revive latent negotiating skills. However, there is also the need to ensure that the buyer marshals maximum negotiating power in the first place. This will be dissipated if different parts of the company are separately negotiating similar but smaller deals, or if the total value of the business to the supplier is underestimated.

Negotiating manoeuvrability is also reduced, and hidden costs potentially lurk, if there is an *over-focus on price and inadequate assessment of total cost of ownership.* The total cost of purchasing anything is much more than the initial price. Delivery costs, payment terms, 'extras' and training are all examples of factors which have financial impact. Not realising this, the buyer runs the risk of accepting the lowest price from those offered but finds that additional charges lead to higher total cost. Smart buyers also take account of the time value of money. One company was faced with two similar bids for a major Capex project, but the suppliers made different proposals about the phasing of payments. Discounted cash flow analysis showed a clear preference for the supplier who asked for the bigger payments later in the project. Ignoring this would have meant paying too much too soon. Negotiating effectiveness is also at risk if too few negotiable variables are on the table. The more there are then the easier it is to avoid deadlock. In these cases, one party might resist on one topic but will concede on another, thus enabling the buyer to achieve a result that is acceptable overall.

The term 'soft money' is rarely used. Unsurprisingly it is the opposite of hard money. Hard money describes things like unit price, delivery charges, hourly rates and so on. Soft money is more difficult to pin down as it applies to things that are valued but not so easily quantified. *Ignoring soft money* risks extra costs. Take the case of a maintenance contract. The user will have confidence in an existing supplier who already does a good job but may charge more than a potential alternative. 'In any case the alternative supplier would be cheaper, wouldn't they, just to get the order?' For as long as costs are not put on them, soft money factors such as confidence and scepticism will always win. It keeps the user in their comfort zone. So, what would increase user confidence if the cheaper source was considered? The customer's maintenance supervisor could be assigned to them for two weeks to show them the ropes and keep an eye on them until confidence is established. Now add this supervisor's cost to their bid. This quantifies the value that is put on 'confidence'. Other soft money factors can be similarly added in. If the total adjusted cost of the alternative bid is still less than the current incumbent's then there is a solid case for change. Sticking with the status quo just consumes money unnecessarily and risks loss of profit.

Inappropriate or poor Supplier Relationship Management occurs if buyers feel that their job is complete once the contract has been placed. Inferior contract performance, added costs, claims, and delays are just some of the potential risks. These risks were discussed in Chapter 2 but they are mentioned here to emphasise that the procurement process must continue to be effective after contract award and is not complete until the supplier's work is finished and paid for. Resources, routines, and responsibilities have to be allocated accordingly.

In past times *asset disposal* was a minor consideration which only became an issue a long time after the asset was acquired and by which time it had become totally obsolete. This has changed since product life cycles have shortened dramatically (potentially leaving obsolete assets with a much higher residual value), plus heightened awareness that assets should be recycled or otherwise disposed of in an environmentally and socially responsible manner. The risks of getting it wrong include failure to turn residual value into real money and law suits and reputational damage if disposal protocols are violated. Smart buyers know that asset disposal should be treated as reverse procurement, thus benefiting from the disciplines and rewards of that process.

All the above risks are present in a company where procurement activity is regarded as the province of a few buyers who have a short term focus and are frantically employed operating the mechanics of the supply chains whilst ensuring that order-placement procedures are satisfied. The way forward is to raise procurement's profile and increase its influence across the business in tactical and strategic terms.

The journey starts with understanding markets better and training the buyers. Traditional procurement departments know about market prices and potential sources but typically do not *analyse how the supply market works under the surface.* Enlightenment starts by understanding how the supplier's costs build up to the asking price; where the product is in it's life cycle; and what the supplier's intentions are for this product's development or phase-out etc. Analysis then goes deeper to understand who are the primary players in the supply market; how viable they are; and what mainly influences market movements in price and capacity. The best question a buyer can ask is 'why does this happen?' As a minimum, buyers' questions reduce the risk of nasty surprises and gain insights which increase negotiation effectiveness.

Under-trained personnel can be found in all phases of the procurement process: from commercially naïve requisitioners who are easy prey for sales tactics; through buyers who lack influencing and negotiating skills and do not have the decision-making tools and data infrastructure to engage in anything like strategic activity; to finance people who do not understand that playing non-payment games destroys supplier goodwill. The fact is that training for buyers alone is not enough. In most companies, comprehensive management of the risks inherent in the procurement process require nothing less than a transformation in procurement's identity and influence in the company.

PRINCIPLES AND RISK PREVENTION

Business today poses tough questions. Procurement can provide many of the answers but often is not positioned to do so effectively, if at all. If you are in business then you are in procurement and exposed to supply side risk. Unless your company is happy to settle for inferior processes, then doing procurement properly is not discretionary and not a function whose activity is sized according to how many cost savings can be made. Procurement's business role is to contribute to company strategy, then distil out its supply implications, and then act to make strategy happen. Procurement's task role is to create and sustain the supply markets the business needs for it to succeed now and in the future.

Traditionally, procurement-risk considerations have always been part of a good buyer's repertoire, but only as facets of specific procurement tasks. In 1983 Peter Kraljic[6] advocated the risk-management necessity for 'Purchasing to become Supply Management' but it has taken the business world until relatively recently to acknowledge PRM as a business topic in its own right. There is no doubt that the whole is greater than the sum of its parts. The maxim that 'brakes were invented so that cars could go faster' (although it was probably the other way round) is often cited as the positive reason for risk management. Risk management is not so much about

---

6   Read more about Peter Kraljic and his breakthrough Portfolio Analysis in Chapter 7.

stopping things from happening as it is about being able to operate, safely, at new limits. A company with high class risk management will be able to do things that lesser companies cannot. Thus a procurement process that has comprehensive risk management principles at its heart, will be able to acquire more value from its supply markets, and be caught out less often, than would traditionally be the case.

The future of procurement as a core business process depends on how successfully it overcomes perceptions about its role which stem from the past. The elevation of procurement on the CEO's agenda is often due to the realisation that a major profit contribution can be made, and a cost-reduction promise is a perfectly acceptable reason for awakening interest. But a change programme has to reach beyond being a specific cost-reduction *project* and instead aim to transform procurement into an ongoing *process* of value acquisition and risk management.

Box 3 shows familiar, though not necessarily sequential, steps along procurement's re-positioning journey. Initially the object is cost savings (steps 1–4), then cost management (steps 5–9), leading to sustained value acquisition (steps 10–15).

'*Cost Savings*' is essentially a leverage game which can be deployed by procurement teams with little involvement from others in the company. '*Cost Management*' sustains the initial gains made from cost savings, and then recognises that other strategies have to be employed to gain further benefits. Continuing to leverage cost reductions is futile and strong suppliers will not be interested in this game anyway. Whilst '*Sustained Value Acquisition*' is built on a sound cost management foundation, it has a fundamentally different orientation. The difference concerns procurement's role and

BOX 3

TWO JOURNEYS TO THE SAME DESTINATION

1. Push harder on existing deals.

2. Add similar deals together   "Route 42"

3. Get the licence to make more profound change   starts here

4. Standardise to create more and larger deals.

5. Improve contract and risk management.

6. Evaluate deals versus total lifetime 'hard/soft' cost.

7. Develop simple supply strategies.

8. Position procurement as a core business process.

9. Improve specifications.

10. Create commercially aware cross-business teamwork.

11. Develop collaborative supply relationships.

12. Establish '5-star' Procurement Risk Management.

13. Increase influence over monopolies and cartels.

14. Penetrate areas of non-traditional procurement.

15. Develop far-reaching supply strategies.

reach. 'Supply costs' are not viewed negatively but as essential pre-requisites for trade in the first place. In this scenario, procurement is seen as an intrinsic fact of being in business rather than an activity to support someone else when they have said 'buy'.

What is less evident, in practice, is the parallel journey, referred to in Box 3 as Route 42. For the mathematically inclined, '42' comes from a process-transformation template where a score of seven represents excellence in six aspects of the procurement effectiveness.[7] The key is to recognise that proceeding stepwise along the roadmap requires more and more people to be involved in the journey. If the bus only has procurement people on board then it will stop at cost savings. Procurement cannot be a service and strategic at the same time. It only has the potential to become strategic when it is accepted as a shared process spanning across, and from top to bottom of, the business.

The two parallel journeys respectively deliver financial benefits, reduce exposure to risk and re-position procurement's role. This ensures that cost-reduction activities break through the barrier that is reached when cost savings dry up. Route 42's destination is the profitable survival of the company deriving from a high-performing, sustainable procurement process which is positioned and managed as a source of corporate vitality. The same goals apply to a public sector organisation although the financial focus will be on sustained viability rather than profit.

---

7   The six aspects are procurement's contribution and influence; relationships; procedures and audit framework; organisation; infrastructure and systems, and staff resources.

Step 3 in Box 3 means redefining procurement's role and stating the principles that clearly apply to all people whose work impinges on the procurement process, not just the buyers. Put very simply, procurement's role is to ensure that the company acquires maximum value from the supply markets it needs to ensure profitable survival … and that they *are* there in the first place. Further, and no matter how decentralised or delegated the procurement action is, the CPO needs to have ultimate authority and control over the process whereby the company interacts with these markets.

CEOs need convincing before they agree to any of this. A good place to start is to tell the familiar story of how cost savings contribute to profit, but take care to judge what their current perceptions might be and start from that point. These might be that he or she sees procurement as being:

● unnecessary;

● a regulator of the order-placement process;

● there to achieve lowest prices;

● expected to make cost savings;

● managing costs and supply risks;

● a contributor to successfully achieving corporate strategy.

Purchasing Power[8] describes how to make procurement's case from each of these starting perceptions. Talk about

---

8 *'Purchasing Power'* R.C. Russill, Pearson Education, ISBN 0-13-442625-8, page 32ff.

procurement using the language of the boardroom, and not the vocabulary of an arcane backroom function. Supply markets are increasingly used as sources of competitive advantage and as means of achieving strategic objectives. This is not just about reducing the cost base but about attracting other forms of value. Examples include increasing top line sales by constructing order-winning bids with supplier collaboration, and also taking the time to figure out where a potential customer's procurement activity is in 'maturity' terms vis-à-vis best practice, and then approaching them accordingly. Attracting supplier-led innovation is increasingly necessary for profitable survival, as is receiving preferential treatment during supply shortages and protecting margin when supply prices rise but customers force discounts. In this context, strategic procurement is not so much a definition of tasks done in an intelligent and forward-looking way, but a means of deploying a powerful competitor-beating organisational capability.

In his book *The Empty Raincoat*,[9] Charles Handy describes the horizontal S-shaped Sigmoid Curve, a concept particularly relevant to procurement at this time. Handy explains 'the Sigmoid Curve sums up the story of life itself. We start slowly, experimentally and falteringly, we wax and then we wane. It is the story of the British Empire, and of a product's life cycle, and of many a corporation's rise and fall. Luckily there is life beyond the curve, the secret being to start a new "up" curve before the first one peters out. The right place to start the second curve is when things are going well and still "on the up". That would seem obvious were it not for the fact that all the messages coming through are that everything is going

---

9   'The Empty Raincoat' Charles Handy. Published by Arrow Business Books, 1995.

fine. However, we usually wait for a downturn, when we are looking disaster in the face, before making change.'

And then it is too late. The vehicle for procurement's transformational journey, fuelled by cost savings but now running on empty, ends at the terminus. The next bus is about to set off on Route 42 and the next S-Curve. What must we do to make sure we are on that one instead?

FURTHER QUESTIONS FOR URGENT ATTENTION

- Is our CEO likely to ask the question 'are we doing procurement intelligently?' If this happens, how will we answer it? If it is unlikely that this question will be posed, what can we do to stimulate it?

- Do we have a policy that governs the receiving of supplier visitors by non-procurement personnel and which reduces the risk of commercial unawareness?

- Do we exhibit any symptoms of a flawed procurement process?

- If so, then the need for immediate actions will be self-evident. But how can we ensure that these actions are not just knee-jerk solutions to a problem but also move us towards building a better procurement process?

- What stage have we reached in Box 3's improvement journey? What must we do to take the next step?

(5) Management Controls

The value of procurement fraud in the UK rose by 347 per cent in 2008.[1] And the outlook is that there will be more as recession-hit companies slash costs and cut controls as well. Despite these omens, another survey[2] found that only one-third of respondent companies were taking greater steps to mitigate procurement fraud.

However, economic hard times are not the only reason why the risks of internal fraud will increase. Companies' reliance on technologically-managed financial transactions is now so great that enormous frauds can be perpetrated at the flick of a switch, enabled by lax controls and driven by greed. Speaking in 2002[3] the then chairman of the US Federal Reserve, Alan Greenspan, observed 'it is not that humans have become any more greedy than in generations past. It is that the avenues to express greed have grown so enormously.'

So, more risks lurk in the area of Management Controls. In 2005, the Office of Fair Trading encouraged whistleblowers

---

1   *Supply Management*, 11 June 2009.
2   *Supply Management*, 19 March 2009.
3   *The Daily Telegraph*, 17 July 2002, 'Fed slams infectious greed of business'.

to highlight corruption in the supply chain. This advice was obviously taken to heart as, later in that year, the buyers in two London boroughs were in the news for 'taking payments'. Whilst these may not have brought the Boroughs concerned to their knees, Barings Bank suffered a rather more spectacular fate in February 1995 as a result of weak management controls that allowed rogue trader activity. However, the business world does not learn. In January 2008 French Bank Societe Generale took a hit of 4.9bn euros from a trader hoping to loot money whilst everyone's eye was off the ball watching the world's unfolding economic crisis. What bank traders and company buyers have in common is that they both have access to, and deal in, the company's money. The topic of management control is therefore highly relevant to PRM but the whole area is one that is rarely understood and applied in business to the extent it needs to be. However, fraud is only one aspect of it and even the most honest of company staff can unwittingly hurt the company by their actions in the absence of effective controls.

Management Controls cover the principles; procedures; authorities, and checks and balances that the company relies on to guide and influence peoples' behaviours as they go about their business. As one firm puts it: 'Control comprises all the means devised by an organisation to direct, restrain, govern and check upon various activities. Its basic purpose is to see that business is conducted in accordance with management's directives, in pursuit of corporate objectives, and with due regard for the interests of shareholders and the public.' To which another successful firm adds 'we are convinced that there is a correlation between good control and efficient operations.'

Examples of potential risk situations are:

- unworkable or inappropriate procedures;

- biased selection of 'three-bid invitees' and over-reliance on favoured suppliers;

- unofficial and unauthorised commitments to contract;

- breach of confidentiality;

- internal fraud and 'backhanders';

- corrupted tender evaluation;

- abuse of commitment authority and call-off agreements;

- invoices paid twice or not at all; payment for goods not received;

- unchecked price increases;

- failure to benefit from volume price-breaks;

- failure to control the letting of leases;

- over-control;

- speculative buying;

- flawed authorisation of contract changes and claims.

RISKS AND REMEDIES

In fiercely task-oriented companies there will be great emphasis on stating *what* a job-holder is expected to do, but this is very different from describing *why* a job-position exists. Today's leaner organisations, and the greater delegation of decision-making authority which needs to go with them, mean that people must be able to see how what they do links with the ultimate goal of the company.

Delegation of authority can bring great risks if there is no framework for it; if people do not know their authority limits, and if there are no checks and balances (witness the above bank failures). The procedural route is one way of dealing with this, but *unworkable or inappropriate procedures* might force behaviours which expose the company in other ways. The classic example is where a company insists that for any contract above a certain monetary value (and this is usually set too low) then three competitive bids have to be sought. This rule is based on the perfectly sound idea that buyers should search out the best offer available before placing their business. It also ensures that the eventual decision is transparent and objective and not made with any unacceptable bias. (Interestingly there is often no corresponding rule that defines how to construct the list of suppliers who will be invited to bid, and hence the risk of bias still exists.) If a market is genuinely competitive, and if the value of the order merits it, then the three-bid approach is fine. However the approach fails if the supply market is distorted. In the case of a monopoly the procedure is unworkable, and it is totally inappropriate for cartels where it is exactly the approach they hope for. The answer is to set out clear policies and principles which give the buyers the central reference points around which to construct specific approaches appropriate to the situation being dealt with.

Procedures can be useful as they stop time being wasted re-inventing the wheel for frequently encountered situations. But to insist that they be applied with mindless disregard for real life exposes the company to significant wasted costs.

Arguably, the risk of *biased selection of 'three-bid invitees' and over-reliance on favoured suppliers* should be discussed in Chapter 4, Procurement Process. However, it is included here since it is important to have good controls as well as good policies. This is because the three-bid policy can be manipulated so that the buyer's preferred supplier comes in with the best quote. How? Simply by nominating as the two other bidders suppliers who are known, maybe from a recent bidding exercise, to bid high. Suppliers would do this if, e.g. they were already too busy and did not wish for this business, or if they are tired of being included on bid lists just to make up the numbers. Incidentally, disinterested suppliers will prefer to bid rather than not bid at all as this latter stance may well exclude them from being invited to bid in the future. Thus the buyer effectively continues a sole-nominated source policy which on the surface looks like competitive sourcing and satisfies the auditors. That said, there is the need for a balanced approach because it is also good practice to place a repeat order with a recently engaged supplier if the buyer believes that a new bidding exercise would lead to the same result and thus be a waste of time. The problem comes when the bias persists. The risks in these practices are that the buyer drifts away from competitive costs and reduces sourcing options because other potential suppliers lose interest. The controls' answer to this is to have 'forensic' data analysis systems signalling when a trend of biased supplier selection persists.

A serious controls' risk encountered in many companies is where a budget holder wrongly assumes that their authority to decide what a budget should be used for also means that they can decide with whom the money should be spent, and 'how'. The risk materialises as *unofficial and unauthorised commitments to contract*. This means that a budget holder may say something like this to a supplier: 'Look, I've decided that we need you to make these parts for us but we need them urgently. Can you please get started? Meanwhile I'll get the buyer to formalise things with an order.' The speaker has now exposed both his or her own company, and the supplier, to many risks. A recent case involved the supplier 'getting started' and incurring costs. The customer then cancelled the instruction. The supplier sued and won, the judgement being that the supplier had every reason to assume that the budget holder had the legal authority to commit, whereas this was not the case.

One of the most fundamental principles of control is the 'segregation of duties'. In a procurement context this means that one person has the authority to decide how a budget should be utilised ('requisitioning authority'); another has the legal capacity to commit the company to a contract ('commitment authority'), and a third has the authority to pay money ('payment authority'). Once clearly defined and allocated, it is possible to merge some of these authorities under controlled conditions. But allowing them to be combined by default is the recipe for controls' chaos.

Information is power and companies often weaken their position by allowing valuable information to seep out of the company. This might be a knowing *breach of confidentiality* or the unwitting transmission of buying signals. The former loses the company a competitive or strategic advantage and the latter reduces negotiating power. It is therefore necessary to define what information is company confidential and what is not, and also to alert people across the business to the commercial sensitivity of the things they might say even if not an outright breach of confidence. The company's policy on confidentiality also needs to prescribe how confidential data is classified and how it must be disposed of when no longer needed. This especially applies to the disposal of tender documents and supply agreements which, in the wrong hands, reveal commercial information useful in future negotiations and bid submissions. And do not forget invoices. A recent High Court case[4] found an ex-employee guilty of stealing invoices from his old firm and passing them to a rival company after he lost his job. The judge ruled that the case satisfied the three elements of a breach of confidence: that the information was confidential; that the staff member had no right to pass it on; and that the recipient company had made use of the information. Whilst this case involved customer invoices there are similar sensitivities where supplier invoices are concerned.

Confidentiality controls should also cover details about internal organisational structures and who in the company possess what authority. Unwitting release of this information allows sellers to aim more accurately for their targets, and unscrupulous sales representatives to claim familiarity with senior managers in order to persuade junior personnel to take actions which would otherwise seem doubtful (see Chapter 3 and invoicing scams).

Deliberate release of confidential information, especially if in return for money or other benefits, raises the topic of *internal fraud and 'backhanders'*. Without appropriate controls it is possible for corrupt personnel to buy things for their own

---

4   *Out-Law News*, Out-Law.com, 17 June 2009. High Court judgement dated 12 June 2009.

use; to accept excessive hospitality or bribes from suppliers who are then rewarded with contracts; and to use company purchasing agreements for their own benefit, even if they use their own money to do so. The vast majority of buyers are ethical and well-motivated so, rather than ring fence them all with prohibitions, it is better to understand and deal with the causes of dishonest behaviour in the first place. Controls experts know that three ingredients are necessary for fraudulent behaviour to be possible. These are: an initial motivation (e.g. the desire to hurt the company or an abnormally high need for money); incentive (high potential gains and low risk of detection); and opportunity (e.g. easily circumvented controls or predictable checks by management). If all are present then the company is exposed to internal fraud or malpractice.

The risk of *corrupted tender evaluation* has already been raised in the chapters on Market Conditions and Behaviours (highlighting the risks of cartels and information brokering) and on the Procurement Process (unequal or unfair application of the tendering process giving rise to lawsuits from unsuccessful tenderers). It bears further mention because proper controls around the tendering process will reduce these exposures. Smart companies distinguish between bid clarification, bid conditioning and post-tender negotiation. Clarification is the process which ensures that every aspect of the supplier's offer is correctly understood. Conditioning is the process which brings the different bids onto the same basis so that apples are compared with apples. These processes reveal the successful supplier who is advised accordingly. The company's policy may then be to allow post bid negotiation only with this supplier, the object being to see if the deal can be improved to mutual advantage. A further control is to reject late bids.

Although not fraud, it is possible to *abuse commitment authority and call-off agreements*. Normally a buyer will have commitment authority up to a certain monetary value. For a potential order above this value they will have to seek commitment approval from a more senior colleague as prescribed in the delegation of authority framework. If the value is £100k e.g. and the buyer's limit is £50k, then the buyer can progress things without further reference by placing two contracts of £50k each. It might be a lack of time which causes this, or simply that the buyer wishes to avoid an onerous review of options with the boss prior to getting approval. Either way, the company is committed to an expense which probably did deserve higher review. If the buyer's authority is too low anyway then this is not an excuse to abuse it. In this case the authority level should be revised upwards as part of an objective periodic review of the delegation framework. Call-off agreements are commonly found where raw materials, spare parts or services are purchased regularly. They are commercial arrangements where supplier and customer have agreed on a pricing and performance structure and which anticipate that a certain volume of business will be placed in a given time frame. As with one-off purchases, they can be abused if the buyer splits a large requirement into smaller ones in order to avoid higher-level review.

The risks that *invoices might be paid twice or not at all and that payment is made for goods not received* are self-explanatory. However this does not stop these mistakes happening. The risk of paying for non-performance is usually countered by checking that there is a match between the invoice and goods-received note before authorising payment. Equally obvious is the risk of *unchecked price increases* but, given the creative ways that suppliers can introduce price rises by stealth, it is understandable that some of these can get past ineffective controls. If a supplier is selling a range of different items there is nothing illegal about constantly adjusting some prices and not others; bundling items into special deals, and making big unit-price reductions on small volume items whilst applying small increases on high-volume parts with the net effect being to increase total revenue. PRM involves ensuring that buyers are aware of these and other tactics, and that controls are in place to ensure that changes in invoiced prices are not accepted until approved or rejected by the buyers concerned.

In good times and when firms are busy it is easy to miss the fact that volumes purchased have risen above expected levels with the result that the customer *fails to benefit from volume price-breaks*. Many contracts, whether for unit-priced material items or hourly-paid services, offer better rates at higher volumes. A volume-to-price check should be part of the normal payment controls' process and a review of total business done should always precede annual price negotiations. If volumes have declined then the buyer needs to be ready with other arguments which extol the virtues of his or her custom and so repel pressures for cost increases. A price rebate can often be negotiated retrospectively if volumes have been better than expected but were not recognised at the time.

Failure to control the letting of leases can create onerous liabilities for a company, especially if the authority level given to a buyer is the same for committing to leases as it is for letting purchase orders or supply contracts. The risk here is not so much the value of the lease as the time for which it commits the company. There have been examples where company 'x' has been acquired by company 'y' and the latter has been saddled with an un-needed and unwelcome lease commitment it inherited. This risk is lessened if it is only a designated senior manager who has authority to agree to leases in excess of one year's duration.

Over-control can be just as damaging as under-control. This de-motivates the jobholder as virtually nothing can be done without approval from a higher authority. The risks are that work becomes slipshod because someone else is effectively checking it; delays occur; rules or procedures might be abused just to make it possible to get the work done, and time wasted on trivial work means that strategic issues are neglected. One company[5] estimates that 75 per cent of its buyers' time is sucked into dealing with a high volume of mechanistic work, with only 25 per cent of time being devoted to expensive strategic supplies being sourced from difficult and risky supply markets. Over-control can also stifle a buyer's talents which then never see the light of day The answer is to devolve some tactical commitment authority to users; create call-off contracts for them to access directly, and adopt technologies such as procurement cards.

Another step is to see if the buyer's authority can be increased, or if indeed it is being correctly used in the first place. A junior buyer in a medium-sized engineering company had all the right ideas for getting suppliers to be more productive and for locating new competitive sources. However, her time was almost completely consumed by mechanistic order-placement processes. First, the rules stated that three or more competitive quotes had to be obtained for any potential purchase order > $800, and yet the buyer applied it to everything. This self-imposed discipline certainly erred on the safe side but was an unproductive use of time since the savings made did not repay the cost involved. Analysis showed that 77 per cent of the

---

5   'Purchasing Power' R.C. Russill, Pearson Education, ISBN 0-13-442625-8, page 69.

total orders she placed could have been placed without three-bid enquiries. More time was then spent getting the purchase order approved because the CFO's signature was required for all of them. This rule reflected the company's need to control outward cash flow. A better control would have been to set a maximum total of dollars which could be spent via small purchase orders during a given time period and have the buyer schedule and approve things accordingly, knowing that the company's record of commitments thus made would be part of the management's regular operational review.

Speculative buying usually ends in financial embarrassment. It occurs when the buyer believes that it is a buyer's market and commits to purchase more volume than is currently required in order to capitalise on the never-to-be-repeated bargain prices. The risk is that the company is left with large volumes of unwanted stock which can only be disposed of at rock-bottom prices. Lean manufacturing disciplines demand that orders are only placed when the planning system, suitably informed about prevailing lead times, triggers purchase-order placement. However, market prices do fluctuate and are certainly not guaranteed to be at their lowest when the company's planning system demands action. One control would be that, even though the manufacturing plan has not yet called for the raw materials, forward orders can only be placed if the buyer knows that their company has a customer for the finished product. It is then a judgement as to whether the cost advantage of ordering 'now' is greater than the added cost of storage and earlier payment.

Contract management is a controls' minefield and a subject in its own right. Basic terms and conditions of contract are certainly necessary for assigning responsibilities to buyer and seller, but do not often anticipate what happens when real life intrudes. Chapter 2 examined how some contractors may seek to extract more money from clients by making aggressive claims for 'extras'. *Flawed authorisation of contract changes and claims* occurs when the person authorising a legitimate claim is the same person who authorised the contract in the first place. The risk is that, if the claims are accepted, the final cost of the contract can end up being higher than the authority limit of the buyer concerned.

PRINCIPLES AND RISK PREVENTION

The above risk examples, although not exhaustive, reveal the diversity of expensive and damaging events that happen when the procurement process is not controlled in an enlightened and knowing way. Companies that force-fit their procurement process into rigid procedures are really saying that they do *not* trust the buyer but *do* have unquestioning faith in the competitive workings of the supply market. Operating instructions which give the appearance of tight control are often wide open to manipulation by suppliers who find it easy to read a predictable game plan. Further, buyers may feel forced to circumvent unfriendly procedures just to get the job done. Many managers think that controls are a sign that people are not trusted and are an unwelcome bureaucracy that stops things happening. The opposite is true and it is better to think of controls in the context of flying an aircraft. Controls are what you use to make things happen the way you want them to, and they are essential to running a well-managed business.

Business controls are vital, but will only be effective if they are seen as practical and relevant to the business exposure. Simple examples of controls are the separation of responsibilities between budget holder or user (requisitioning authority) and buyer (commitment authority); review and approval of negotiating targets; contract terms and conditions, and goods received/invoice payment checks. High class companies start by trusting their buyers and by being wary of the supply market in general. Then, typically, they increase buyer commitment authorities by quantum leaps and not by small adjustments to keep pace with inflation. To put a limit on personal authority is not suggesting that the buyer cannot be trusted with more, it simply matches decision-making *capacity* with proven decision-making *capability*. As buyers grow in experience, so more authority can be passed to them. However, many companies deny buyers the authorities which they are well able to use. The challenge here is to persuade management that 'delegating more authority' is not relinquishing control, but rather replacing outmoded controls with modern alternatives consistent with the demands of business and the reality of a very complex and dynamic global supply environment.

In the risk area of management controls, prevention is definitely better than cure. But rather than try to anticipate every transgression and prevent it before it happens it is better to create a culture where transgression is not contemplated in the first place. Best practice PRM focuses on key principles and policy which influence the decisions and behaviour of *all* those involved in the procurement process, not just the buyers. The CPO then looks for compliance with these core principles instead of demanding slavish adherence to procedural detail. These principles deal with the following topics:

1. Business ethics and corporate business practices.

2. Authority and separation of responsibility.

3. Budget holders' authority to requisition.

4. Legality and commitment authority.

5. Form of contract (including terms and conditions).

6. Supplier performance management.

7. Custody and disposal of assets.

8. Payment authority.

9. Joint procurement with other companies.

10. International sourcing.

11. Source dependencies.

12. Purchasing from other Group companies.

13. Confidentiality.

14. Use of Approved Suppliers and Qualification.

15. Enquiry types and formality.

16. Statutory reporting.

17. 'Best Value' basis for tactics and selection.

18. 'Face Value' policy.

19. Documentation.

20. Approach tactics (bidding, negotiating, etc).

21. Contract award.

22. Relationship between functional and business lines.

23. Early involvement of procurement personnel.

24. Dealing with supplier visitors.

25. Company image in the supply market.

26. Supplier relationships.

27. Contract administration.

28. Delegation of commitment authority to users.

A short guide cannot go into further details but the value of the list is that it questions whether or not a company states its position on these issues. Ideally this requires a stand-alone statement for on each policy rather than having a detailed procedure which reflects correct thinking but does not explicitly define it. The 'reach' of this policy list is revealing. Items 1–8 are basic controls of business practice; items 9–16 control procurement practice within the business overall; items 17–21 specifically deal with the search for best value, and items 22–28 embrace all company personnel in the procurement process. A European benchmarking survey[6] showed that the cost management performance of companies who were working to the entire policy list was 400 per cent

---

6   Private research by author in conjunction with the Juran Institute, Europe.

more effective than those whose policy reach stopped at number 16.

Trust is the key to company high-performance and effective controls. Onerous procedures do not provide it. In 2009, UK politicians were besieged by public opinion scandalised by abuses of the parliamentary expenses system. As one news commentator observed: 'The problem was not an absence of rules. It was that there were so many rules that they crowded out any space for judgement or the exercise of individual morality. Free individuals encouraged to act ethically are more likely to arrive at the right answers than an over-mighty bureaucracy.' In procurement, trust without control is naively irresponsible; control without trust is self-defeating as de-motivated individuals will beat the system, but trust with principled control empowers people and transforms their effectiveness.

FURTHER QUESTIONS FOR URGENT ATTENTION

- Do our procurement policies and controls apply to all company personnel spanning right across the business? … or do they only control the actions of buyers and are hidden away in our general finance policies?

- When and how were our procurement policies last reviewed? Do they reflect the current expectations of the business and regulatory worlds?

- Have our procurement policies been formulated with the involvement of someone who understands supply market behaviour and contractual risks?

- Do we always invite supplier offers in the same predictable way?

- Have we ever departed from our rules for inviting and evaluating formal tenders? If so, why was this done and who authorised it?

⑥ Handling the Unexpected

One stormy evening, the power supply to a semi-conductor plant in New Mexico was knocked out by a lightening strike. This stopped production. Whilst this may not have been a totally Unexpected Event, one telecoms company reacted quickly in line with its procurement risk management plans. Interestingly, they were first alerted to the event by their supply-chain monitoring systems which flagged up delayed shipments from the production plant. The problem deepened and the telecoms company successfully locked in alternative sources of supplies. It thus avoided significant damage to its profit, compared with a less-agile competitor who failed to react and suffered huge financial losses.[1]

Meanwhile, in another business sector, a food company assessed the vulnerabilities in its supply chain for chicken.[2] Disease was identified as a possible event of at least medium probability. Contingency plans were laid. Salmonella struck and the company seamlessly switched to 'plan B'. A competitor, faced with the fact of zero supplies, had no option but to buy chickens from the company with the 'plan B' supply chain.

---

1   *The Economist*, 17 June 2006. 'Being lean and mean is a dangerous thing'.
2   Private conversations with the company concerned.

The well-prepared food company not only sustained its own production but was also agile and entrepreneurial enough to seize the opportunity to make additional profit from sales to its competitor. Neither the telecoms nor the food company could foretell the future but both were demonstrably better at responding to it when problems occurred.

This chapter deals with a company's ability to Handle the Unexpected so that it survives the disruptions and resumes its progress towards desired goals. Success depends in part on the culture and agility of the company team and partly on being able to demonstrate that 'chance has favoured the prepared mind'.

Examples of potential risk situations are:

• failure to anticipate potential events;

• over-reliance on predictive tools;

• no strategy or master plan to provide a frame of reference for dealing with unexpected events when they occur;

• ad hoc reactions to events which diminish public confidence in the company's ability to manage in a crisis;

• delayed or deficient responses which allow better-prepared companies to secure competitive advantage;

• rigid autocratic management styles which paralyse company personnel and prevent people from using personal initiative and expertise at ground level;

- a 'helpless' mindset.

RISKS AND REMEDIES

Whilst some events may be genuinely unexpected there will be others that could realistically have been foreseen. Unstructured, or an absent, risk assessment increases the likelihood of *failing to anticipate potential events* so that risks remain unidentified. Another cause is an incomplete or corrupted analysis of historical data. A Zurich Report in Applied Risk Management[3] cites the tragic accident that befell the Challenger space shuttle as a result of the failure of seals. Analysis of previous failures focused on six out of 24 incidents whereas it would have been more appropriate to include all incidents in the statistical analysis. The probability of future failure would then have been calculated to be much higher under the launch conditions on the day. The reference does not seek to cast blame but highlights the danger of not letting past data tell the whole story. We also fail to anticipate potential events if we are not creative enough in imagining what they might be or, if we are, then to dismiss them prematurely.

The risk of smoothing out past data creates *over-reliance on predictive tools*. Calculating things to three places of decimals gives a false impression of infallibility. In his book *Fooled by Randomness*, Nassim Nicholas Taleb[4] develops the theme that it is a human tendency to do this, that we try to explain past events using logic and looking for patterns of cause and effect. In doing so we ignore, either subconsciously or by eliminating 'spikes' in the data, the effect of randomness and chance.

---

3   Zurich Financial Services Group, *Zurich Insight 01*, 2008.
4   *'Fooled by Randomness,'* Nassim Nicholas Taleb, Penguin 2007.

Creative risk identification and exhaustive data analysis might reclassify otherwise unforeseen events as being distinct, albeit unlikely, possibilities. However, it is wise to assume that genuinely unexpected events will occur even if it is not possible to put a label on them. These are more difficult to handle if there is *no strategy or master plan to act as a frame of reference for dealing with them* if and when they occur. It is easy to be rendered helpless by an unexpected supply-related event, and not quite know how to respond to it. This is waiting for the future to call the shots. It is far better to believe in shaping the future and to create strategies to get there for each key item or service required from the supply market. The general benefit of strategy is that it not only anticipates 'what if' scenarios but it also means that plans are already being acted on. This gives the organisation momentum. In his book *Making it Happen* the late Sir John Harvey-Jones refers to momentum as being crucial so long as it is allied to a strategy which creates the sense of direction. As he says, 'you can alter direction more easily on the move than you can if you are static and if you have set the direction in this way it will almost alter itself.'[5]

Strategic planning imposes the discipline of thinking things through beforehand. This in turn reduces the occurrence of *ad hoc reactions to events*. If it looks as though a company is reacting to events as they occur it diminishes public confidence in its ability to manage in a crisis. Reactions and statements become inconsistent and, instead of damping down the fire today, they provide fuel for hotter public scrutiny tomorrow. The company is shown to be unprepared, or worse, to have no robust strategies and processes in place for managing its affairs in general. It is also surprising how few companies provide media training for the senior managers who can find

---

5   *'Making it Happen,'* John Harvey-Jones, Fontana 1989, page 64.

themselves in the front line confronting hungry journalists. Basic training includes developing the politicians' skill of handling (and often not answering!) probing questions and knowing how to survive the pressure of the interview studio. It is fundamentally important to have two or three key messages to put across given the opportunity of the public platform. Although it may be an adverse event that causes the publicity in the first place, the skilled media operator will not only avoid unwittingly admitting liability but will take the opportunity to score positive public relations points in the process. These only work if they are genuine as the public is quick to detect insincerity.

Strategy is no good if it never leaves the drawing board. Swift and decisive deployment will head off the risks of *delayed or deficient responses which allow better-prepared companies to secure competitive advantage*. The presence of strategy, contingency plans and momentum is only part of the story. It also matters that people in the company have permission to act and can link their individual actions to the overall goal. To make this happen involves communicating the big picture and delegating authority. Action-oriented people who cannot see the goal are like unguided missiles. Talking of a crisis time in Coca Cola's history the company's then CEO, Roberto Goizueta, put it this way: 'We needed to establish a sense of direction so that people knew where they were going. Then you can let them have a lot of freedom. But if they don't know where they are going, you don't want them to get there very fast.'[6]

It is also said that, on the eve of the Battle of Trafalgar, Lord Nelson hosted dinner on *The Victory* for his admirals and then got down to the team talk. The overall battle plan was

---

6   *Fortune Magazine*, 11 December 1995, page 52.

discussed and roles allocated. Back on their own ships and in the heat of battle the following day, each admiral was able to take local action which dealt with their specific situation whilst also pursuing the strategy overall. This was possible because the goal had been made visible to them the night before. Not being able to make a telephone call to HQ meant that they needed, and had, the authority to make on-the-spot decisions. The rest is history.

The converse of this is that *rigid autocratic management styles paralyse company personnel and prevent people from using personal initiative and expertise* at ground level. More than a good framework of management control is required. Leadership style also comes into the equation. Sir John Harvey-Jones has his observations on this as well: 'the difference between good managers and bad is that the good have the ability to create and manage the future.'[7].

Inspirational leaders also have the ability to create a culture of High-Performance Teamwork (see later in this chapter). These teams get things done. The opposite is a *'helpless mindset'*. Comparisons like this link with the fact that some people are deemed 'lucky' whilst others are not. I recall conversing in Hong Kong with a highly accomplished Chinese businessman who claimed that his success depended on 'luck'. This did not seem credible and his answer needed probing. Our 'analysis' revealed that success depends on:

---

7   *'Making it Happen,'* John Harvey-Jones, Fontana 1989, page 125.

Hard work	75%)
Charity work (giving peace of mind)	10%) = 'planned luck'
Listening to the fortune man (Feng Shui)	10%)
'Pure luck'	5%
Total luck	100%

This tells a different story: that 95 per cent of his success came from what he called 'planned luck'. Another business lady, also from Hong Kong, told me her own definition of planned luck ... 'luck is where preparation meets opportunity'. The Asians know a thing or two about luck but perhaps it was Louis Pasteur who also hinted at the 'planned luck' idea by noting, in the context of experimental observation, that 'chance favours only the prepared mind.'

Despite the consistent theme that being prepared does help one to handle the unexpected, there are further indications that the right attitude is also useful. Psychologist Richard Wiseman has researched why some people get all the luck while others never get the breaks they deserve. His research[8] identifies four characteristics of the lucky mindset. People who have this:

• are skilled at creating and noticing chance opportunities;

• listen to intuition;

• imagine success which helps them to create self-fulfilling prophecies;

---

8   *Skeptical Inquirer*, The magazine for science and reason, Vol. 27, No.3, May/June 2003. 'The Luck Factor'.

- are resilient and think positively in the face of adversity.

There is a plausible, if untested, connection between these observations and those of the Chinese businessman: doing charity work involves doing something different with different people (increasing the likelihood of chance opportunities) and feeling able to act on the advice of the Feng Shui man must depend more on gut feel and intuition than on logic.

Such conclusions invite agreement from those who are lucky, and dismissal from those who are not. Thus, even the definition of 'luck' comes under the microscope but this does not move the debate forward. What matters is that it seems eminently desirable to exhibit these characteristics or to learn how to acquire them. The burden of proof should be on those who argue the opposite. Everyone can look back at bad things that have happened in their life and think they are unlucky. The choice is between dwelling on these and defining oneself permanently by them, or to draw strength from coming through such travails and look positively to the future. See the film '*My Big Fat Greek Wedding*' and take as a motto the line 'don't let the past dictate who you are. Let it be a part of who you can become in future.'

PRINCIPLES AND RISK PREVENTION

The first step towards being able to handle the unexpected is to make the unexpected smaller. The 'unexpected' category only includes those potential events that do not have a label on them. So the more labels that can be written, the smaller the number of their unlabelled cousins.

Creativity techniques can help to imagine the impossible. By nature the human individual is creative but much happens during development, both at the hands of parents and education systems, to inhibit it. For example, school teaches us to work out 'the right answer'. Convergent thinking confines the search for risks within the box of past experience: 'what problems might occur?' By contrast, creative thinking asks 'how many ways can we think of to create problems?' A European oil company successfully used this technique to identify hitherto unexpected ways in which raw material could be lost from the supply chain. Instead of the usual question 'where are we losing crude oil?' between the oil rig and refinery tankage, they took the creative route and said 'let's imagine we're an oil molecule ... now, how many ways can we think of to escape?' Many were found.

It can be both useful and entertaining to consort with futurologists. Whilst some come across as astrologers in pinstripe suits there are other organisations who employ disciplined and structured approaches. These do not predict the future but instead scope out its possibilities based on underlying trends. Such companies make it their business to watch what is happening in the world. Tuning into their observations is one way of demonstrating the lucky person's characteristic of watching for, and being open to, opportunities. We do not have to accept a futurologist's view of the future but we can use their scenarios to prompt some 'just supposing' and 'what if' analyses. Mathematical predictions can produce more scenarios to be tested but it is dangerous to take spuriously accurate calculations as evidence that things will definitely happen that way. We cannot extrapolate from the past to predict the future. All this does is provide a baseline which shows how wrong we can be. What this and the above does do, however, is to bring hitherto unlabelled events out into the open. And once they are there we can decide what risk management strategy, if any, will be employed.

The benefits of strategy have been described earlier but what should they, and strategic procurement, look like? The strategic procurement job involves much more than just testing the market for best prices and dealing with contract and order placement. Procurement is strategic when:

- its activities are directly linked to the main goals that a company is striving for, rather than being a back-room function dealing with contract and order administration;

- it believes that supply markets can be changed so that their behaviour (in terms of cost, supplier performance, and supply security) is what the business needs it to be, and it knows how to change this behaviour;

- it is clearly understood in the company that procurement is a cross-company process which embraces a number of different business functions, the incumbents of which are able to play a commercially aware role and appreciate that their behaviour can affect, for better and worse, the results achieved.

A good strategy must then pass the 'Grove' test. This is an acronym defining the characteristics of an acceptable strategy. First it has a **G**oal, that is, a clearly defined future desired state of the supply market. Then the strategy is **R**elated to the core strategies of the business as well as to specific financial and operational targets in the time periods covered by the strategy. It is **O**rchestrated, both in its development (by cross-functional teams) and its execution (by a strategy 'leader' with other appropriate personnel singing from the same hymn sheet). The strategy is **V**isionary … it is about 'change' and being ambitious enough to stretch for the 'unreachable'. It is not about accepting the status quo as being the best that can be done. Finally it **E**xtends beyond current deals made in the current year. Any deals made 'today' to meet a current need are also taken as opportunities to take a step closer to the desired future state.

When they occur, unplanned events can be evaluated against the template of the strategy, which in turn becomes the launch pad for turning a crisis into an opportunity to advance the strategy. But is the organisation agile enough to do this and does it have the 'lucky' culture? The most value-oriented, resilient companies do not limit their attention to tangible assets; they also focus extraordinary effort on developing intangible assets such as unique business practices, a strong brand and organisational knowledge.[9]

Based on their research of a number of business and non-business teams, James A. Ritscher Associates[10] have defined the characteristics of high-performing, spirited organisations as follows:

- clearly stated vision and purpose;

- strong collective alignment with that vision and purpose;

- culture and organisation shaped to support the purpose;

- authority delegated as low as possible;

---

9   Business supplement: 'Risky Business,' *Daily Telegraph*, 17 September 2005.

10   James A. Ritscher Associates, 1983, 1060 Beacon Street, Brookline, MA 02146, USA.

- a lean and simple structure;

- hierarchy kept to a minimum;

- dedication to the professional growth of employees;

- people treated as professionals: empowered, trusted, competent;

- support for innovation and ideas for change;

- toleration (but not duplication) of mistakes;

- teamwork instead of in-fighting;

- high emphasis on ethics and integrity.

There is also some evidence that high-performance teamwork needs to extend outside the organisation as well as within. Research by global consultancy and services company Accenture[11] showed that companies investing in Supplier Relationship Management programmes achieved three times the cost effectiveness of companies who did not. Companies who achieved most of their procurement benefits from post-contract activity were labelled SRM leaders, and these positioned their supply chains as a strategic capability. Such companies may not be more successful at predicting the future but their supply chain mastery enables them to respond more quickly to market place changes. The notion that the buyer-seller relationship already has momentum and has the same goals echoes Sir John Harvey-Jones' conclusions about the value of strategy.

---

11   *Supply Management*, 15 December 2005.

If we tie all of this to the 'lucky' mindset we have the following:

- are skilled at creating and noticing chance opportunities

    - getting out and about, e.g. visiting suppliers rather than vice versa
    - inviting help from suppliers ('how can you help us meet this need or solve this problem?') rather than instructing them what we want them to do
    - striving for intelligent accountability[12] rather than mindless box ticking

- listen to intuition

    - empowering people, whilst ensuring that the skills and management controls are in place to give confidence in the use of delegated authority
    - focus on principles and values as central terms of reference for delegated activity, rather than ring fencing it by onerous procedures
    - trust
    - ensuring that people know the goal and the big picture

- imagine success which helps them to create self-fulfilling prophecies

    - having strategies which pass the GROVE test

---

12   BBC Reith lectures, 2002. Baroness Onora O'Neill. 'A Question of Trust'.

- believing that external situations and events can be influenced rather than meekly accepted

- are resilient and think positively in the face of adversity

    - tolerating mistakes so long as learning accompanies them
    - internal mentoring and regular personal appraisal
    - in the heat of the moment not losing sight of the end game and ultimate goal

In an uncertain future where actions need to be rapid, dependable, imaginative and effective, forecasting can scope out the risks and possibilities, but human commitment and resourcefulness is what counts when dealing with whatever actually turns up. The future belongs not to those who seek to predict it or to repeat the past, but to those who have the capability to deal with whatever the future will throw at them ... and especially to those who have the ability to make 'planned luck'.

FURTHER QUESTIONS FOR URGENT ATTENTION

- Do we have a reporting system for classifying and learning from supply chain failures that we have experienced in the past?

- Do we use creativity techniques to imagine and label potential supply disruptions?

- Do we have Supplier Relationship Management plans in place with key supply partners?

- How many of the twelve characteristics of high-performing teams do we exhibit? If we do not measure up, why is this and should we change?

- Do we provide media training for senior managers including the CPO?

(7) Procurement Risk Management – An Integrated Approach

PROCUREMENT RISK MANAGEMENT IN ACTION

The purpose of this guide so far has been to focus on the 'impact' component of the risk management equation:

$$\text{Being 'At Risk'} = \text{Impact} \times \text{Probability} \times \text{No Mitigation}$$

$$\text{where Impact} = \text{Exposure} \times \text{Event}$$

with special emphasis on searching out potential risks lurking in five risk landscapes:

1. External Dependencies

2. Market Conditions and Behaviours.

3. Procurement Process.

4. Management Controls.

5. Handling the Unexpected.

Specific risk events, and the means of dealing with them, have been illustrated to show how different the landscapes are, as well as emphasising the fact that risks exist inside the organisation as well as outside in supply chains and supply markets. The philosophy of this guide is that truly effective PRM requires the organisation to have a process for working things out and also to possess a culture and operating framework in which risk management is systemic and as much a part of daily activity as is turning up for work in the first place. Hence, each chapter sets out the principles of risk prevention relevant to the landscape concerned.

So, thus equipped, how do we put PRM into action? Here is the outline process:

1. Gather data about current supply expenditures.

2. Decide which supply categories are particularly important to examine first.

3. Involving a cross-functional team, identify potentially disruptive events for each supply category, looking at the supply arrangements from the perspective of each of the five points of the Risk Catcher in turn.

4. Assess the impact of each event if it happened, along with the probability of it occurring.

5. Focusing on those events which are deemed likely to occur and which will have harmful impact, devise contingency plans or take actions to reduce the pain or probability.

6. If the selected actions are only able to manage risks in the short term, set in place supply strategies designed to manage or reduce the 'at risk' situation in future.

7. Regularly monitor external and internal events to see if risk alerts need to be escalated, and every three months re-visit and refine the overall risk analysis and its management conclusions.

HOW TO GO ABOUT PROCUREMENT RISK MANAGEMENT

Each of the above steps is now examined in more detail:

STEP 1: GATHER DATA

This involves compiling the list of active suppliers; how much the company is spending with each of them and what items or services are being purchased. Supporting information includes data about trends in prices and costs; volumes used and how these are expected to change in future; current supplier performance and any changes in their demeanour or circumstances and any events planned or otherwise expected, such as price reviews or contract renewals. Consider also the importance of the company's products and services which rely on these supplies.

STEP 2: DECIDE WHICH SUPPLY CATEGORIES TO EXAMINE FIRST

The first task is to sort expenditures into categories. A 'category' is a logical group of related items or services coming from a supply-market sector where suppliers operate in similar supply chains and value-adding processes. A category is named after the item or service provided, not the names of the supply companies involved. For a Kraljic analysis (see below) less than 20 categories would be too few and more than 35 too much.

A category that accounts for > 5 per cent of total supply spend is too large and should be divided into two or more smaller groups. For example, 'Information Technology' would be too big a category on its own, either because the supply chains go back to quite different sources (e.g. hardware manufacturers or software designers) or because the total expenditure on IT exceeds the 5 per cent threshold. Contract services such as 'Hotels and Travel' or 'Facilities Management' would be two different categories because of the different competencies needed. The competence is related to the core activity of the supplier. For example, in Hotels and Travel the supplier understands how these markets work and has access to preferential deals and journey planning tools; whilst Facilities Management is about organising and deploying various teams and applying programme- and project-management skills.

The second task is to apply a Kraljic portfolio analysis.[1] This is a four-box matrix devised by Peter Kraljic in 1983 and

---

1   *Harvard Business Review*, September-October 1983. Reprinted with permission in CPO Agenda, Autumn 2008, along with an interview with Peter Kraljic by Dick Russill and Philip Usherwood to celebrate 25 years of Procurement Portfolio Analysis.

which has magnificently withstood the test of time. The grid is framed by an x-axis called 'complexity of supply market' and y-axis labelled 'importance of purchasing' … low to high in both cases. To quote Kraljic: 'the complexity of the supply market (is) gauged by supply scarcity, pace of technology and/or materials substitution, entry barriers, logistics cost or complexity, and monopoly or oligopoly conditions' whilst 'the strategic importance of purchasing (is defined) in terms of the value added by product line, the percentage of raw materials in total costs and their impact on profitability, and so on.' Whilst Kraljic's approach was mainly focused on manufacturing businesses its applicability to service-related activities is proved by the fact that 'portfolio analysis' is as relevant and powerful today as it was when launched.

The most critical quadrant is top right which Kraljic labelled 'Strategic'. Then in descending order of criticality came 'Bottleneck' (bottom right), 'Leverage' (top left) and 'Non-critical' (bottom left). It is interesting to note that for many years up to the present, the prevailing and wrong, justification of procurement's raison d'etre has been that it exists to make cost savings. However, Kraljic's emphasis was on risk management. And in conversation with him in 2008 to celebrate the twenty-fifth anniversary of his original paper, cost savings were not mentioned at all until towards the end of the interview. How quickly and effectively the sight of money, or the prospect of spending less of it, obscures what procurement is really about![2]

From a PRM viewpoint it is obvious to concentrate first on those categories residing in the Strategic and Bottleneck quadrants … strategic because of the high cost of these categories and

---

2   See Chapter 4, section headed *'Principles and Risk Prevention'*.

the company's reliance on them, and bottleneck because they too are mission-critical and supply markets do not offer much, if any, choice of alternatives.

Finally, map the selected category supply chains as flow charts which show how items, or service provision, reach you from the supplier and the supplier's supplier.

STEP 3: IDENTIFY POTENTIALLY DISRUPTIVE EVENTS

Having assembled the above data, most procurement teams could easily proceed with the following steps as well. But this would be a lost opportunity. First, it will ignore the risk perspectives of other company colleagues, especially those on the receiving end of supply chains. Second, it will not open non-buyers' eyes to the reality of the company's exposure to its supply markets and the need to manage them properly. The minimum team would number, say, five and involve people from procurement, finance, users, a relevant technical specialist, and the company's risk manager, if there is one. Also engage, as required, the risk-management expertise already available in the company in the form of:

- insurance advisers;

- finance people;

- equipment inspectors;

- IT and knowledge-management specialists;

- quality teams;

- legal advisers;

- internal auditors.

The procurement leader does not have to know as much about specialist areas as the specialists do. What is vital is that they know when to tap into the expertise they need and then make decisions and provide leadership for subsequent actions. This highlights the CPO's role as a key ingredient in the company's leadership team as distinct from managing a support activity. In some companies it has been found that the cross-functional event was the first time that such a team had been brought together. A small step for PRM but a big step for cross-company collaboration!

Given that people are busy with other things it is wise to select just one or two supply categories for the first meeting. This ensures that time permits a worthwhile risk analysis and will also whet participants' appetites to return for more in the future.

For a selected supply category, define what is at risk or 'exposed', putting a monetary value on 'units of disruption'. For example, if a production process has to be stopped because of the absence of raw materials, then what is the daily cost of downtime? If the price of a commodity raw material rises by 'x' per cent then what is the cost of lost profit? If an outsourced data-processing service fails to perform what is the cost of lost productivity? Focus on the costs of disruption or loss, not the disruptive event itself.

Display the relevant supply chain flow charts and add any modifications or facts contributed by the team. Supply chain mapping is guaranteed to reveal information about what is happening, and where, that was not previously understood. Even that lack of knowledge is an 'at risk' situation. The same approach can be used to map the processes of procurement decision-making and management control relevant to that supply category.

Look at the flow charts and, for each exposure that the team has listed, question how it might be damaged if a disruptive event occurred in each of the five Risk Catcher landscapes. For example:

- Our reputation and brand as a responsible company is exposed to the actions of others (internally and externally). How many potentially harmful events can we imagine might occur in each of the following risk landscapes?

  - external dependencies (e.g. unethical sourcing practices by a key supplier)
  - market conditions and behaviours (e.g. being an unsuspecting victim of illegal cartels)
  - procurement process (e.g. failing to meet statutory procurement requirements; not honouring contractual commitments)
  - management controls (e.g. commitments exceeding expenditure authorities; speculative buying)
  - handling the unexpected (e.g. no strategies; no effective media-savvy emergency response teams)

- Our financial performance is exposed to cost levels and to cost trends. How many potentially harmful events can we imagine might occur in each of the following risk landscapes?

- external dependencies (e.g. poor supplier quality; supplier bankruptcy)

- market conditions and behaviours (e.g. volatile commodity prices, supply shortages)

- procurement process (e.g. over-specification; commercial unawareness)

- management controls (e.g. abuse of competitive bidding; unwitting acceptance of price-increase stealth tactics)

- handling the unexpected (e.g. supplier terminates a newly-agreed contract and imposes 47 per cent price increase on spot purchases).

In compiling these lists of events, draw inspiration from past experiences (including those that might be dismissed as random); find out from press reports what is happening elsewhere, and think creatively to imagine the impossible. Do not assign probabilities at this stage or dismiss suggested events as being implausible.

STEP 4: ASSESS IMPACT AND PROBABILITY

Some companies get along perfectly well by assigning 'high,' medium', and 'low' ratings to an event's impact and probability. This gives a 3×3 risk-management grid where the events falling into the high risk 'red' quadrants require urgent attention; those in the 'amber' area need contingency plans; whilst those deemed as 'green' are acceptable risks albeit needing periodic monitoring to confirm that they stay 'green'. However, a 3×3 grid is quite a coarse mesh which can lead to risks being over- or under-managed. A 5×5 grid provides finer control without getting too detailed. Whilst there is no substitute for organisation's working things out for themselves, the axes could be defined as follows, using the convention 1 = low and 5 = high:

Impact:
- Minimal (1)

    - impact can be contained by flexing operational plans and budgets with no eventual loss of money/time, etc. Such impacts can be labelled 'accommodating the event with no loss'

- Minor (2)

    - impact of the disruption can be contained within local plans and budgets (e.g. a local company within a group) but another activity or expense has to be cancelled or deferred to accommodate it. Such impacts can be labelled 'accommodating the event by displacement'

- Moderate (3)

    - revenue of the organisation is decreased
    - significant impact on costs and operations ... may turn a profitable activity into a loss
    - loss of customer(s) or competitive advantage
    - financial losses are met by arranging funding from elsewhere in the company group or from extra borrowing
    - event requires internal investigation
    - company leadership probes what happened and demands response plan

- the outside world does not hear about the event and is not interested anyway

- Major (4)

  - as 'moderate' but with negative public-relations impact
  - reputation tarnished
  - company share price takes a hit
  - incident leads to government inquiry or regulatory probe

- Catastrophic (5)

  - company or organisation collapses or is taken over.

Probability:

- Remote (1): may occur but only in exceptional circumstances (one event in 25 years)

- Unlikely (2): not expected to occur in normal circumstances (one event in ten years)

- Possible (3): event might occur at some time (one event in five years)

- Likely (4): will probably occur at least once (one event expected in two years)

- Almost certain (5): will occur in most circumstances (one event expected in one year).

STEP 5: FOCUS ON EVENTS REQUIRING ACTION TO REMOVE 'AT RISK' SITUATIONS

Each category examined will have its own 5×5 grid and, following step 4, each event can be assigned to a box relevant to its impact and probability. Risks rated with a score of 15 or more are in the 'red' zone and require urgent action to reduce impact or probability. Risks with scores between five and 14 are in the 'amber' zone. Although they may be allowed to materialise, their impact is lessened by deploying contingency plans. 'Green' zone events are deemed acceptable but their possibility is kept under review to ensure that circumstances do not change such that the risk is escalated.

Risk management actions fall into two categories: 'Direct Actions' reduce or eliminate the impact of disruptive events, whilst 'Indemnity Actions' are designed to compensate for loss if it occurs.

Examples of Direct Actions are:

- reducing likelihood and consequences (e.g. reduce commitments, option contracts, inventory stockpiles);

- diversification (e.g. multiple sourcing);

- standardisation to reduce dependence on unique sources;

- changing policies and procedures;

- sharing risks and opportunities;

- bringing in-house a previously outsourced activity;

- implementing additional controls or audit programmes;

- implementing strategies to develop supply markets so that they become 'less risky'.

Examples of Indemnity Actions are:

- insurance;

- buying forward and hedging;

- laying the ground for legal settlement (e.g. performance bonds, penalty clauses);

- back-to-back contracts where, at the input end of the business, a supply contract's term and commercial elements are mirrored in a customer contract at the output end.

A company's risk manager should be conversant with the range of direct and indemnity options available in general, but it will be the CPO's expertise that is needed to expose supply-related vulnerabilities in the first place and to gauge the impact and probability of events. And then, of course, to provide leadership and accountability for subsequent PRM actions.

STEP 6: PUT RISK-REDUCTION STRATEGIES IN PLACE

The value of having 'a strategy' was set out in Chapter 6 (Handling the Unexpected). The benefits are twofold. Partly there is the argument that a company that is implementing strategy is more agile and adaptable to events as it is already on the move and so has momentum. The second benefit is what the strategy actually delivers in terms of changed circumstances which serve the company better than the current situation. These actions can be classified as direct actions, albeit highly strategic ones which may impact on the company's structure or business model. It took an overnight price hike of +30 per cent for a critical raw material, and an equivalent and immediate plunge in profitability, for one company to learn the hard way about its exposure to a hostile supply market. Then followed some serious risk analysis and strategic planning, one element of which was to vertically integrate by buying a medium-size supply company making this raw material. This reduced the company's exposure to greedy prime suppliers. Similarly, a company feeling vulnerable to far-distant low cost sources might plan to develop an equivalent domestic supply capability. Any higher cost could be viewed as an insurance premium providing peace of mind about supply reliability.

STEP 7: REGULARLY MONITOR EXTERNAL AND INTERNAL EVENTS TO SIGNAL RISK ALERTS

Nothing stands still and change happens quickly. Having faltered late in the previous year, the 2008 global economic roller-coaster took barely five months to plunge from the heights of 'boom' to the depths of 'bust'. Smart companies re-visit their Kraljic analyses at least once every six months and survey their risk landscapes more frequently. In addition, they remain alert to events around them, sensing their impact on the business. The timings of US presidential elections and Olympic Games are well-known in advance, but weather patterns are less predictable. That said, companies with regional and global supply chains monitor weather forecasts, geological surveys, pandemic outlooks and the like in order to pick up impending natural disasters before they materialise as unexpected disruptive events. Closer to home, negotiating schedules will show periods of heightened industrial unrest at ports or in airlines when temporary supply chain stoppages might occur. The key is to pick indicators specific to a category's supply chain and monitor them.

Given current economic woes, many companies are rightly concerned about a supplier's viability. Credit checks are useful but no longer enough as they focus on the way things have been as distinct from what might happen tomorrow. The priority now is to gather fragments of information and assemble them into a mosaic that tells a picture ... good or bad. A PRM plan that picks up some or all of the following signals will be providing early warning of impending supplier failure:

- supplier shortens credit lines;

- cash discounts offered for early settlement;

- invoice factoring;

- delayed payments to own suppliers;

- insolvencies of tier 2 suppliers and onwards;

- news that supplier has lost major contracts;

- quality problems and reduced delivery accuracy;

- major purchases deferred;

- lack of CAPEX on mission-critical equipment;

- overdraft facilities exceeded;

- wages not being paid;

- concentration on short-term deliverables to raise cash;

- increased borrowing just to keep business running;

- funding comes from clever and innovative financial products;

- changes in management and staff and rapid turnover;

- company accounts and other filings delayed.

It is important not to attach too much weight to any one piece of data. What counts is the overall picture and the direction of trends. None of the above data will usefully be obtained by sending supplier questionnaires. Frequent visits to the supply company and other forms of regular contact are required, and the good news is that the buyer does not have to do it all. Other non-buyer colleagues have these contacts and, if they are primed to look for the warning signs, then data capture will be all the more comprehensive.

The same 'mosaic' approach applies to the other risk landscapes. Take for example, a company's internal processes where so-called forensic accounting techniques will pick up untypical and possibly fraudulent expenditure patterns or abuse of delegated authority. Here are some tell-tale signs:

- advance payments to suppliers;

- dormant supplier accounts becoming active;

- bogus invoices 'raised' by suppliers with whom the company no longer does business;

- dummy invoices;

- overpayments;

- duplicate payments;

- supplier address same as employee address;

- changes or corrections on invoices.

GETTING BETTER AT PROCUREMENT RISK MANAGEMENT

The four states of PRM maturity can be described as follows:

1. *Ignorance:* putting one's head in the sand and hoping that things will be alright.

2. *Awareness:* risk identification comes from asking 'what if?' questions; being streetwise and creative; learning from past incidents, and knowing where to look ... helped by addressing all five points of the Risk Catcher.

3. *Evaluation*: assessing impact and probability in a structured and consistent way.

4. *Risk Management:* appropriate measures are in place to contain or mitigate impact or to compensate for loss, plus regular reviews and receptiveness to supply chain alerts.

These general labels can be expanded using the Self-Assessment and the Risk Catcher to map out a PRM improvement plan. Figure 7.1 shows the Risk Catcher again but now with two profiles added. The 'dark grey' line indicates a typical current situation, and 'light grey' the desired end state. Data for the dark grey line comes from an ongoing series of field surveys conducted by the author in public and private sector organisations. It records participant companies' self-assessment of PRM preparedness. The emerging theme is that organisations are assessing themselves as being similarly prepared (albeit still some way off from maximum) for risks in the areas of External Dependencies, Management Controls and Procurement Process. However there are lower scores for Market Conditions and Behaviours, and Handling the Unexpected.

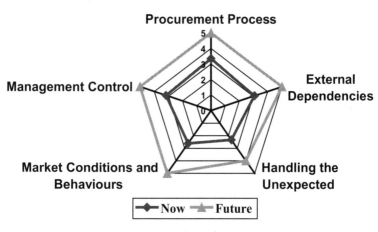

Figure 7.1   Towards PRM excellence – closing the gap

This possibly reflects the journey that procurement is making in many companies, namely changing from an internally-focused well-controlled task function into an outward-looking business-management activity with strategic intent.

How would we recognise PRM-excellence in practice? Here are the key criteria:

- 'no hiding place for risks': the search process is comprehensive and creative;

- the search for risks covers all supply spend;

- impact is quantified: there is a focus on what is at risk (i.e. exposed) and the cost of disruption when undesirable events materialise;

- probability is assessed at least semi-quantitatively (i.e. 5×5 grid);

- actions and strategies are regularly reassessed and adjusted;

- a 'world watch' is maintained to keep an eye on potential events (external and internal);

- there is time to do it.

Chapter 4 argued that effective PRM requires more than the deployment of certain techniques. For most companies the additional challenge is to transform the company's procurement process into a core activity. The 'two journeys with one destination' are advocated both there and in Purchasing Power.[3]

The result will be culture change as well as cost and risk-management effectiveness. As one CEO put it: 'the procurement process is a microcosm of the whole business and if I can achieve high-performance in that process then this will be the catalyst for achieving high-performance in the business overall.'[4]

Certainly there are other processes which run right across the business but what is unfortunately different about the procurement process is the lowly status with which it has come to be regarded by businesses in general. Why that is so is another story, but its being a fact means that to improve attitudes towards it requires near superhuman efforts on the part of those advocating change, and massive re-thinking for the whole corporate team to 'buy in' to the fact that their roles and behaviours may need to change in future. It is the pain involved which makes the cure such a positive and lasting one.[5]

---

3   'Purchasing Power' R.C. Russill, Pearson Education, ISBN 0-13-442625-8, page 76.
4   Private discussion with President of Asia-Pacific operations of multinational company.
5   'Purchasing Power' R.C. Russill, Pearson Education, ISBN 0-13-442625-8, page 66.

Index

If you have found this book useful you may be interested in other titles from Gower

A Short Guide to Operational Risk
David Tattam
Paperback: 978-0-566-09183-4

A Short Guide to Political Risk
Robert McKellar
Paperback: 978-0-566-09160-5
e-book: 978-0-566-09161-2

A Short Guide to Ethical Risk
Carlo Patetta Rotta
Paperback: 978-0-566-09172-8
e-book: 978-0-566-09173-5

A Short Guide to Reputation Risk
Garry Honey
Paperback: 978-0-566-08995-4
e-book: 978-0-566-08996-1

Visit **www.gowerpublishing.com** and

- search the entire catalogue of Gower books in print
- order titles online at 10% discount
- take advantage of special offers
- sign up for our monthly e-mail update service
- download free sample chapters from all recent titles
- download or order our catalogue